Cooking with Spirit

Written by Jasmine Rose

Outskirts Press, Inc.
Denver, Colorado

Outskirts Press, Inc.
http://www.outskirtspress.com

ISBN: 978-1-4327-2736-9

Outskirts Press and the "OP" logo are trademarks belonging to Outskirts Press, Inc.

PRINTED IN THE UNITED STATES OF AMERICA

This book is dedicated to my son Chris, who
at times, believed in me more than I believed in
myself and who understood my greater vision for
Cooking with Spirit and also to my daughter-in-law
Leah, who helped me with what seemed like endless
technical difficulties.

ACKNOWLEDGEMENTS

Over the past eight years, <u>Cooking with Spirit</u>, has become a friends and family project. A special thanks to the Woo-dee-woos who have tasted, tested and edited many of the recipes. Karen, Phyllis, Madonna, Sharon, Betty, Mary Ann, Katie and Es, I love you all so much. Es, thanks too, for all your help with the pictures. I'd still be trying to get the fuzz out if it weren't for you.

An enormous hug goes to my husband Tim, who has eaten every single recipe in this book over and over again. You are my MAIN TESTER, sweetie. Thanks too for the nights when I threw a quick sandwich at you so I could keep working. You never complained.

Jim and Jenny, endless thanks for digging through the Martin-Nicol archive to find the long-forgotten pictures we used in the book. Your continuous love and support made the process so much fun.

Grateful appreciation to Rose D'Antonio who showed me how important it is to cook from scratch. Rose, you will never know how much of an inspiration you have been to me. Thanks for everything.

To my Grandma Hattie and my Grandma Elsie who taught all of us how important it is to gather family around to eat wonderful, home-cooked food. To Susan and her Mom, Esther Tilley, who always have extra space at holiday dinners. To my Dad, who made the best scrambled eggs on the planet. He taught me how to be creative with food. To my Mom, who let me go crazy in the kitchen once in awhile.

Last but not least, to all of my grandkids. I hope I have inspired you to cook because it's fun, to laugh because it makes you feel good, to share because we can and to know beyond a shadow of a doubt there will always be a big hug for you and a new adventure the next time we get together.

Thanks all of you from the bottom of my heart and the tips of my toes.

TABLE OF CONTENTS

VII. Soup

INTRODUCTION

This is more than a cookbook, it is more than a labor of love - it is a prayer for humanity. When I first started writing these recipes down almost eight years ago, I had no idea they were going to turn into a cookbook. I just wanted to remember some of the incredible ideas for meals that were popping into my head.

I have cooked since I was twelve, to help my mother. She had a husband, four kids and a full time teaching job. A lot of us understand this and can honestly say, been there - done that. From the very first, I couldn't leave a recipe alone. I was constantly experimenting and loved the way any food could be prepared and presented, so it would look like a gorgeous, colorful, edible painting.

After I had written down about 30-40 of these recipes, I started directing my energy to assembling them into a cookbook, but a very different cookbook. I took one ingredient from each recipe and made a list of them. I used that list to learn about the history of these foods and how each benefited the body. I discovered, halfway through a mountain of research, THAT WE ARE UNITED BY VIRTUE OF OUR TASTE BUDS!!!! You will see as you go through, <u>Cooking with Spirit,</u> countries from all over the world, many from ancient cultures, have produced and developed the foods you see on your table every day.

If you never make one recipe from this book, it is a wonderful source of information, and if I do say so myself, a cozy book, as well as funny. I love to laugh, a fact that is very obvious as you sit down, with a cup of tea, to scrutinize these pages. The bottom line is this...food is a gift. We need to be celebrating at least one meal each day. We need to give thanks, share with as many as possible, and sit down to talk to each other. Good conversation and wonderful food, wrapped in love and laughter, could go a long way to heal the wounds of this planet. We could rejoice in each other and in that rejoicing see that we are ALL ONE.

Every day we have choices. We can choose to love or we can choose to hate. Wouldn't it be terrific if we could turn weapons (words or otherwise) into hugs? Anger and hatred into love? All we need to do is take the smallest baby step toward love. Invite someone you don't know well to eat a meal with you. Cook something from the cookbook that sounds delicious and fun. Why not have someone cook with you? You can learn a lot about people when you work together. Remember this: somewhere, within every person you meet, is a spark of you. All you have to do is pay attention...notice. "Ahhhh," you say to yourself, "so there you are...don't I know you from somewhere?"

There you have it. The basic reason for putting all these recipes together is to CELEBRATE!!! Celebrate yourself, celebrate your life. When you are grateful for the magic that comes into your life every day, you will see more of it. It is all around you. Noticing the wonder is one of the reasons we are here. Open your heart to the charm of cooking with friends, while wearing fuzzy slippers. Remember what it's like to open your home to guests, serve a fabulous meal, and laugh so much your sides ache. Extend an open, loving hand as often as you can, maybe with a muffin in it. BE JOYFUL, BE GRATEFUL, BE ALL THAT YOU ALREADY ARE!

Here is my toast to the human family ~ Let us give thanks to the Creator for life and the daily pursuit of joy, peace and a good belly laugh. Let us be grateful for the abundance we all deserve. Let us hug instead of hate and always be aware of those sitting at the table with us. Be at peace.

Chapter 1

Fish and Poultry

Watson Park, Chicago, around 1947

NO LEFTOVERS TURKEY TROT
(Serves 4)

It may seem like a lot of ingredients, but this is actually quick to make. Use this recipe when you're tempted to go for fast food or carryout because you worked late and you're pooped. Anyone who is eating with you can help. Before you know it...DINNER IS SERVED.

About 4 T. olive oil
Salt and pepper, divided
½ lb. rotini (corkscrew pasts), cooked and kept warm
4 slices of turkey bacon, cut into small pieces
1 medium onion, sliced
1 small green pepper, seeded and cut into thin strips
1/2 sweet red pepper, seeded and cut into thin strips
1/4 lb. mushrooms, sliced
1 medium zucchini, sliced lengthwise then cut into half moons
4 cloves of minced garlic
1 lb. lean ground turkey, (you could use 2 C. leftover turkey)
2 plum tomatoes, chopped
1 C. sour cream
1 t. dried marjoram or 1 T. fresh

1.) In a large pot, bring 3 quarts of water to a boil. Add 1 T. salt, 1 T. olive oil and the rotini to the water.

2.) While you're waiting for the water to boil, fry the turkey bacon in a large skillet until it's crisp. You might need a little olive oil to keep it from sticking. Remove from pan and set the turkey bacon aside.

3.) In the same skillet heat 2 T. olive oil. Over medium high heat, sauté the onions, peppers and a little salt and pepper together for about 5 minutes. Add the mushrooms and zucchini. Continue sautéing for another 5 minutes.

4.) Remove the vegetables from the pan and set aside. (Don't put the vegetables with the turkey bacon. The hot veggies will make the bacon soggy and we want it crisp.) Heat another tablespoon of olive oil in the same pan. Add the garlic and ground turkey. Sauté until the ground turkey is cooked thoroughly. (If you are using leftover turkey, sauté the garlic in the olive oil for a couple minutes, stirring constantly to keep the garlic from burning. Add the leftover turkey and heat through.) Now put in the tomatoes. Cook for 3 minutes.

5.) Check your pasta. It should be al dente. You have a couple options at this point. You can either drain it or leave it in the pasta water, lid off the pot, until the sauce is ready. The pasta will continue to cook a little but it's an easy way to keep it warm. This is a matter of choice. I'm not a fan of al dente pasta but I don't like it mushy either.

6.) Put the sautéed onions, peppers, mushrooms and zucchini back into your sauce. Heat through for about 3-4 minutes over medium heat. Over low heat, stir in the sour cream, marjoram and crisp turkey bacon. Season with salt and pepper. Do not bring the sauce to a boil or the sour cream might break (curdle), YUK. Just heat through slowly...gently...that's right.

7.) If you haven't done it yet, drain your pasta. Put some rotini on your plate and top with the sauce. Because you have meat, pasta and lots of veggies in one recipe, this can be a one-pot meal if you like. Take a taste. Mmmmm! You did a great job. Aren't you proud of yourself?

****

Unlike a lot of the featured ingredients in this book, turkey is native to North America. The Aztecs and Pueblo Indians were the ones who domesticated it.

It was their variety of turkey that the Spaniards brought back to Spain in 1498.

Today, Europeans prefer turkeys weighing somewhere between 6-10 pounds. Not Americans! Oh no! We like 'em big. If we could find a 40 pound turkey and fit it in our oven, we would. As it is, we have to settle for a tiny 22 pound bird.

I love turkey. Evidently a lot of other Americans do too. The turkey industry in the U.S. produces 100 million turkeys a year, which is a whoppin' 170 times the estimated wild turkey population when the Europeans landed in the New World!!!! Free range, organic turkeys, in my opinion, are the most flavorful and the best for you. There are several farmers near me who raise them but they are getting easier to find in the grocery stores. Ask around...maybe there are some being raised near you.

Since most of the fat in poultry is located in the skin, you can easily remove the skin thereby eliminating nearly all the fat. Poultry is a good source of complete Protein, B Complex vitamins, and Iron. Turkey is very low in Cholesterol and has a respectable amount of Amino Acids which, are the building blocks of digestion. So get out there and eat lots of turkey.

SCARLET O'CHICKEN
(Serves 4)

This is another quick recipe using ingredients you probably have hanging out in your pantry. You know, that can of jellied cranberry sauce you never used at Thanksgiving? Now's your chance to use it up.

Cooking spray
8 pieces of chicken, whatever parts you like
2 cloves of garlic, cut in quarters
Seasoned salt
1 16 oz. can jellied <u>cranberry</u> sauce
Juice of 2 oranges or 1/2 C. orange juice
1 T. water
1 T. soy sauce or liquid aminos*
2 t. Dijon-style mustard
1/2 t. ground ginger

1.) Preheat your oven to 350 degrees. Spray a 13 x 9 baking dish with cooking spray. Place the chicken in the baking dish. With a sharp knife, make a small, deep slit in each piece of chicken. Slip a piece of garlic into each incision.

2.) Sprinkle *lightly* with seasoned salt. Mix the cranberry sauce, orange juice, water, soy sauce or liquid aminos, mustard and ginger together. Spoon over the chicken.

3.) Bake for 60-70 minutes. The cooking time will depend on how big the pieces of chicken are. You can tell if it is done by making a small cut, with a sharp knife, in a thigh or breast piece. If the juices run clear, the chicken is done. If the juice is red you need to bake it for another 10 minutes.

Easy huh? Grab your partner and dance around the kitchen. You have time for a waltz or two. You can make this for company...it is easily doubled. They'll be so impressed and think you worked for hours. Little will they know...you've just been dancing.

*Liquid aminos are like soy sauce but with a lower sodium content. They contain sixteen essential amino acids. I use them as a multi-purpose seasoning. You can find them in a health food store or some of the larger grocery stores.

Early American colonists learned how to make a sweet sauce from cranberries, which grew wild in the Northeast. The Indians ate them raw or dried them in the sun but the colonists boiled them in sugar syrup. This eventually became a part of the traditional Thanksgiving and Christmas dinner. A sandwich made of leftover turkey smeared with cranberry sauce is still one of my favorite "cozy foods." Be careful when you're making your own cranberry sauce, overcooking them makes them bitter. Cook them until they pop and the sauce starts to thicken. That's it.

Cranberry juice is a relatively newer product of the cranberry. Unsweetened juice is helpful many times for people with bladder infections. Cranberries are high in antibacterial and antiviral activity. The juice has to be unsweetened because sugar feeds the yeast which bladder infections flourish on. Makes sense, doesn't it? If cranberry juice straight out of the bottle makes you pucker up too much, dilute it with water, 1 part cranberry juice to 7 parts of water. Then your eyes won't water.

When I was doing my research, I was surprised to learn cranberries didn't have as much Vitamin C as I thought...12.8 mg. per cup. However, fresh have 86% more Vitamin C than canned. Wow!!!! They also contain Vitamin A, Calcium, Phosphorus, Potassium and have no Cholesterol.

I love dried, sweetened cranberries in muffins, scones, sauces, and salads. They make your taste buds wake up and take notice. You go, cranberry!

THE GREAT SECRET OF SUCCESS IN LIFE
IS FOR A PERSON TO BE READY
WHEN OPPORTUNITY COMES. AMEN!

-Benjamin Disraeli

SLIPPERY SALMON WITH A BITE
(Serves 4-6)

People who don't particularly like salmon, love this recipe. My friend Karen says this is the only way her husband, Frank will eat it. Woo-hoo! Eating more fish is fabulous, dahhhling. You can easily cut the recipe in half if you are cooking for two.

2 lbs. of <u>salmon</u> fillets, give or take a few ounces
2 T. olive oil, plus a little for smearing around the jelly roll pan
2 large onions, sliced
Salt

Glaze:
3 T spicy Dijon mustard (if you can't take the heat, use regular Dijon mustard)
3 T. apple jelly, not apple butter
1 T. butter
1 T. fresh lemon thyme or 1/2 t. if you don't have fresh

1.) Put salmon, skin side down, in a jelly roll pan thinly coated with olive oil. Sprinkle salmon with a little salt. Bake at 350 degrees for 10 minutes.

2.) Meanwhile, in a large frying pan, over medium high heat, sauté onions in olive oil until tender and just starting to caramelize (turn brown). Sprinkle a little salt over the onions as you are cooking them.

3.) Put glaze ingredients in a small saucepan and bring to a boil. Boil for one minute.

4.) When the salmon has baked for 10 minutes, remove from the oven and coat liberally with half of the glaze. Top with the sautéed onions and pour the rest of the glaze over all.

5.) Continue to bake for 10 more minutes or until the thickest part flakes easily.

You're going to love this. Salmon is so good, we try to have it once a week, at least. This is luscious with a nice mushroom risotto or the Sunshine Salad...or both if you're really hungry.

I don't serve my family farm-raised fish. I'm never sure what the fish farms are feeding them. I prefer the color, texture and taste of wild-caught salmon anyway. Salmon is found in both the Atlantic and Pacific Oceans. The longer a salmon remains at sea the larger they can become. Makes sense, right? After six winters, a salmon can weigh between 35-45 pounds. The rule of thumb is...the longer the salmon remains at sea and the farther its destination upstream, the better the meal it makes. They have to be caught before spawning though because after that their flesh becomes flabby and yukky. Bears don't mind but, we don't want to be eating no flabby fish.

I can not say enough good things about salmon. It is loaded with Omega 3's which are very good for your heart and your blood vessels. It is one of the foods recommended for high blood pressure. It is a complete protein and contains valuable trace minerals. In addition to that, per 3 oz. piece, salmon has 6.68 mg. of Niacin, 417 mg. Potassium AND 8.2 mg. Vitamin C (that's a lot for a fish). No, I do not own stock in a salmon boat...I just love it and happen to think it's delicious. I can't help it if it happens to be good for you too.

If one person is an expert fisherman, and another an expert at handling a boat, the two working together will catch more than twice as many fish as either working alone.

-John F. Wharton

GINGER CHICKEN OVER FORBIDDEN RICE
(Serves 4)

Forbidden rice is a beautiful deep purple when it is cooked. This is a visually stunning recipe and fabulous for a romantic, evening or when you're trying to impress someone. If you can't find forbidden rice, you can use basmati rice, it's just not as dramatic. At the end of this recipe I will give you information on how you can order it direct, from the supplier.

1 C. forbidden rice
1 3/4 C. water
1/2 t. salt
1 t. honey
1 t. curry

4 T. safflower oil, divided
2 C. broccoli flowerets
1 large sweet onion, sliced
1 medium zucchini, cut length-wise and sliced in half moons
1/2 C. mushrooms, sliced
8 cloves garlic, sliced
2 plum tomatoes, diced
1 T. soy sauce or liquid aminos*

2 T. safflower oil (this is the other part of the divided oil)
1 T. fresh ginger, minced very fine
2 T. peanut sauce**
2 T. soy sauce or liquid aminos*
1 T. honey
1 lb. skinless, boneless chicken breast, cut in small pieces

1.) Put the rice, water, salt, honey and curry into a 3 quart pot. Bring to a boil and reduce the heat. Cook according to the directions on the package.

2.) In 2 T. of the oil, sauté broccoli and onion, over high heat, in a large frying pan or wok. Sauté for 5 minutes. After a few minutes of cooking, add 1 T. soy sauce.

3.) To the broccoli and onions, add the zucchini, mushrooms, and garlic. Continue cooking for 5 more minutes. Add the tomatoes, cook for a couple more minutes. Remove vegetables from the pan; set aside.

4.) Heat the remaining 2 T. oil in the same frying pan. Add the ginger, peanut sauce, soy sauce and honey. Mix thoroughly and bring to a simmer.

5.) Add the chicken and cook for 5-7 minutes, depending on the size of the pieces. When the chicken is done, put the vegetables back in the pan with the chicken. Over a low flame, simmer until just heated through.

6.) Place the rice on a pretty platter. Make an indentation in the middle of the rice like a nest. Put the chicken and vegetables in the indentation. Light the candles and settle in.

WARNING: Do not stir the forbidden rice and the chicken mixture. The color of the rice is so powerful, you will end up with purple chicken, purple broccoli, and purple onions. Hmm!

*liquid aminos can be found at your health food store

**peanut sauce can be found in the Asian section of your grocery store

****

The star of this recipe is <u>forbidden rice</u> but I am going to do a history on rice in general because it is so interesting. I found so much information on its history, I started to get confused. Cultivation began in Asia or India somewhere between 3500 and 3000 BC. Whenever it started, it's very old.

Rice came to the United States by accident. A storm-damaged ship docked in Charleston, South Carolina's harbor for repairs. The captain of the ship gave a small bag of rice to a local planter as a gift. It was a hit. By 1726, Charleston was importing more than 4,000 tons of rice a year.

Rice is a grain belonging to the grass family. Individual plants grow between 2-6 feet tall. Each plant has long, pointy leaves and stalk-bearing flowers which produce the rice grain. Rice is one of the few foods in the world which is entirely non-allergenic and gluten-free.

Forbidden rice, sometimes found at World Market, is grown in China. Legend says it was once cultivated for the Emperor's sole use as a tribute to ensure his good health. It has the most wonderful, nutty almost berry-like flavor. It's hard to describe but it can bring a rice lover to tears.

Rice is naturally Fat, Cholesterol and Sodium free. Today it is grown on every continent except Antarctica. More than 550 million tons of rice are produced worldwide annually. If you have trouble finding forbidden rice, the brand I found is Lotus Foods, website www.lotusfoods.com. It is so worth the extra effort to find this.

SLOBBERING CHICKEN
(Serves 4-6)

The first time my granddaughter, Sara, heard about this recipe she told me it sounded so good, she was slobbering all over herself. She was 8 years old at the time. It was one of those times when you're not sure if your kids/grandkids should see you lose it completely. I laughed so hard my ribs were sore hours later.

2 T. olive oil

1 C. onion, small dice

1 C. celery, small dice

1 med. green pepper, small dice

1/2 t. salt and a couple grinds of fresh pepper

8 skinless chicken thighs

2 15 oz. cans diced tomatoes

1 6 oz can tomato paste

1 C. chicken broth

2 t. dried basil

1 t. dried oregano

4 cloves garlic, crushed

1 t. allspice

1 C. lo-fat cojack cheese, grated

1/4 C. grated parmesan

1/2# angel hair pasta, cooked al dente

1.) In a large frying pan, sauté onion, celery and green pepper in olive oil. Add salt and pepper and sauté for about 10 minutes.

2.) While veggies are cooking, arrange chicken thighs side-by-side in a 13x9 baking dish. *Very lightly* sprinkle with salt. Set aside.

3.) To the veggies, add tomatoes (not drained), tomato paste, and chicken broth. Mix together well. You might need a little more broth, depending on the amount of liquid in the canned tomatoes. It varies from brand to brand. You want a nice sauce, not too thick but not too runny either.

4.) Next add the basil, oregano, garlic and allspice. Blend well. When sauce starts to bubble, reduce heat and simmer 10 minutes, stirring occasionally.

5.) Pour sauce over chicken, making sure all the pieces are covered. Cover with foil. Bake in 350 degree oven for 30 minutes. (While chicken is baking, prepare pasta.) Remove from oven and top with the cojack and parmesan cheeses. Continue to bake, uncovered, for another 20-25 minutes, depending on the size of the thighs.

6.) When you're ready to serve, put a pile of pasta on your plate, put a thigh or two next to the pasta and spoon some of the sauce over the pasta. Serve with extra parmesan cheese and get ready to slobber all over yourself.

****

The featured ingredient for this recipe is <u>pasta</u>. I went on-line to find more information about it's history and found the most fun site. It's www.members.tripod.com/FrancoRossi. If you get a chance, go there and give a hug to Franco.

Anyway, pasta in Italian, means paste. A very long time ago, primitive people learned that grinding grain, mixing it with water, and then drying it, made a food that could be cooked quickly but also preserved the food for a longer time than the grain itself.

It's hard to tell exactly where pasta originated but it is known for sure that Marco Polo did not introduce it to the Italians. He was still in the East when, in 1279 A.D. in Genoa, Italy, Ponzio Bastone was drafting his will and bequeathed a crateful of "maccheroni." Among artifacts discovered in Sicily, were presses for pasta made over 3,000 years ago!

In the 17th century, in Naples, Italy, pasta met tomato, after America was discovered. At this time pasta was eaten with the hands (my grandkids would love that). To the rescue, a chamberlain of King Ferdinand II's, Gennaro Spadaccini, had the idea of using a fork with 4 short prongs. Since then, pasta was served in court.

President Thomas Jefferson, during one of his many trips to Europe, was introduced to pasta. He loved it so much he brought some back to the U.S. and introduced it at one of his famous dinners at Monticello.

4 oz. of enriched spaghetti contain: 422 Calories and 264 mcg. of Folic Acid (being studied for the prevention of certain birth defects). It contains almost no fat, so if you're careful what you put on it, it's really pretty good for you...plus it's yummy. Whole wheat pastas are obviously a little different. They're higher in Fiber, have fewer Calories, less Folic Acid and more Calcium, Phosphorus and Potassium. Then there are pastas made from corn, beets, spinach, rice etc., etc., etc. Happy exploring!!!!

THERE IS NOTHING AS DELIGHTFUL
AS FAMILY OR FRIENDS
COOKING TOGETHER, LAUGHING
AND SHARING THEIR STORIES.

GARLIC AND ROSEMARY ROASTED CHICKEN
(Serves 4-6)

The fragrance of garlic and rosemary nestled inside a plump roasting chicken reminds me of Sunday dinner at my Grandma Elsie's.

1 3-4 lb. chicken	1 T. olive oil
3 sprigs of fresh <u>rosemary</u>*	Salt
8 cloves of garlic, cut in slivers	Pepper
4 large red potatoes, quartered	4 large carrots, peeled and cut in 2"
Some water	lengths

*You can get fresh rosemary in the produce section of your grocery store. Company's coming! YOU! Preheat your oven to 350 degrees.

1.) Get out your 9" x 13" glass pan. Rinse the chicken inside and out. Make sure you've removed the little package of chicken parts from the inner cavity. You can cook them separately and give them to your dog or you can throw them away. Now rub the little bugger all over with the olive oil. Top, bottom, legs...all over. Lightly salt and pepper the inside and the outside.

2.) Place the rosemary sprigs and half of the slivered garlic inside the chicken.

3.) OK, get a small sharp knife with a pointed tip. Pierce through the skin into the chicken and stick in a sliver of garlic. Do this all over the legs, thighs, breast...making at least 8-10 little garlic pockets.

4.) Put the chicken, breast side up, in the pan and fill with 1/2 inch of water (this helps the vegetables to cook but also keeps any fat from spattering all over the inside of your oven). Wash your hands thoroughly with soap to get any chicken bacteria off them.

5.) Arrange the carrots and potatoes around the chicken. Lightly salt and pepper the vegetables. Bake at 350 degrees for 1 1/2 hours. The whole neighborhood will want to come to your house for dinner. The chicken will be a nice golden brown and the skin will be crispy. The legs will move easily when it's done.

6.) Let the chicken rest for 5 minutes to keep the juices in before you start carving it. While it's resting remove the vegetables to a bowl or platter and keep them warm. Carve your chicken...Time for dinner. YAY!!!

****

Rosemary's history has quite a bit of folklore attached to it. All of my research indicated it comes from the Mediterranean, where ancients Greeks wore it in garlands to improve their memory while studying for exams.

For centuries it was thought that rosemary, out of respect, would not grow more than 6 feet in 33 years so it would never be taller than Christ. Another story says that the flowers on rosemary were originally white. The Virgin Mary hung her cloak on a rosemary bush while running from Herod's soldiers with baby Jesus and the flowers turned blue.

In the Middle Ages, people thought if they put sprigs of rosemary under their pillows, it would protect them from evil spirits and bad dreams. It is, however, best known as a symbol of remembrance, friendship and love. Herbal physicians use it topically for rheumatoid arthritis.

Rosemary oil, which you can get at your health food store, is very strong and should never be taken internally. If you want to use it for arthritis aches and pains or just plain old sore muscles, combine 3 or 4 drops in a teaspoon of carrier oil (ie. olive oil or peanut oil) and rub it into the painful area. Ahh! Relief!

You can also make a tea out of rosemary by putting 1 t. of the leaves (which look like pine needles) into a tea ball and pouring 1 C. boiling water over it. Cover and let it steep for at least 10 minutes. Drink up. Add some honey if the flavor is not pleasing to you. This is great for bloating, gas pains, mild gastro-intestinal cramps and arthritis . Five to seven drops of rosemary oil in a tub of hot water makes a great soak...great for circulation and the smell...well...even if you're not a bath person, you've just got to try this. A rosemary bath is also very soothing for crabby, fussy children.

I have always grown rosemary. I tried unsuccessfully to winter it over outside but being from the Chicago area, it is much too tender to survive . So, I grow it in a big pot and bring it inside for the winter. It gets a seat of honor in my bay window. I love cutting fresh rosemary in January and making Garlic and Rosemary Chicken.

It's really easy to grow inside just don't let it dry out. Once a week I take it to my kitchen sink and really soak it with my sink sprayer. It thinks it's getting a bath and usually rewards me by blooming after a bit. I'm growing a creeping rosemary in a pot this year and will try to winter it over too. I'll let you know how it goes.

VERDE SOLE
(Sole Florentine)
(Serves 4)

This is a fast, easy way to make fabulous Dover sole. You say you've never had it! What is it? Well, I can tell you, this sole is not in reference to what is on the bottom of your shoe. It is a mild, delicate fish that is likely to make a fish lover out of your kids.

Olive oil

1 lb. very fresh sole, make sure you smell it before you buy it, unless it's been quick-frozen. If it smells fishy...don't buy it.

10 oz. frozen spinach, thawed, most of the water pressed out

1/2 C. cottage cheese   ¼ C. parmesan cheese, divided

2 T. seasoned bread crumbs   1 T. Dijon or honey mustard

1/2 t. dry marjoram   Salt & pepper to taste

1 T. butter

1.) Drizzle a little olive oil in a 9x9 baking dish. Put the sole in the baking dish. You will have 2 layers. *Lightly* season each layer with salt and pepper.

2.) In a medium-size bowl, combine spinach, cottage cheese, 1 T. parmesan, seasoned bread crumbs, mustard and marjoram. Add just a pinch of salt and some freshly ground pepper. Mix well.

3.) Spread the spinach mixture over the sole. Sprinkle with the remaining parmesan cheese. Dot with pieces of the butter.

4.) Bake, uncovered, in a 325 degree oven for 20 minutes or until the fish flakes easily. Serve hot.

I'm not only going to give you some historical data on mustard BUT, I'm also going to tell you about a fun place to visit if you're ever in the beautiful state of Wisconsin.

As far as I could find out, mustard is the oldest condiment in the world. It is made by grinding mustard seeds, separating the mustard flour from the chaff, then mixing the flour with wine, beer, water or vinegar and finally adding some seasonings. This allows for a lot of creativity in mustard preparation. Mustard paste recipes have been found dating as far back as 42 A.D. Mustard seeds have been found in some of the ancient tombs of the Egyptian pharaohs. You know what I was just wondering? With all the things that are found in those tombs...how was there ever enough room for the mummy? Oh well, anyway, mustard seeds found their way to Gaul, probably via the Romans. By 867A.D., French monasteries were bringing in a pretty good income from the sale of their prepared mustard.

Some of the earliest references to mustard, similar to what we are used to today, go back to the Dijon region of France in the middle 1300's. The French government created strict laws to regulate the methods and ingredients for making mustard to ensure the highest quality. Even today, French law closely regulates mustard production. The French have taken mustard-making to a culinary art.

The English developed their own style of mustard over time. It was originally made at home or in monasteries but not much was sold commercially until the mid-1600's when the town of Tewkesbury became famous for its horseradish mustard. This mustard became the rage in English cooking. Shakespeare loved mustard so much, he referred to the famous Tewkesbury mustard in his play, "Henry the 4th." For reasons unknown, that mustard disappeared from favor. It wasn't until 1804, when the most illustrious name in English mustard,

Jeremiah Coleman, came on the scene. Through skillful marketing, Coleman's mustard became the premium English mustard.

Mustard did not become a hit in the United States until Francis French developed a mild yellow mustard sauce in the early 20th century. It soon caught the public's attention as French's, "Cream Salad Mustard." In the last 30 years Americans have taken to first-rate cuisine thanks to chefs like Julia Childs and James Beard. Grey Poupon, made in the U.S., but with a definite French style, took advantage of this trend and introduced a new variety to the American public. "Ahem, pardon me. Do you have any Grey Poupon?"

Mustard, though usually high in Sodium, is very low in calories and has no Cholesterol. If you like mustard and would like to find some unusual ones, you really need to visit Barry Levenson at his Mustard Museum in Mount Horeb, Wisconsin. He has the largest collection of prepared mustards in the world...over 3,700 varieties!!! There is even an annual National Mustard Day, which is held on the first Saturday in August, at the Mustard Museum. To find out more, you can contact Barry at:

P.O. Box 468, 100 W. Main St., Mt. Horeb, Wisconsin 53572
Phone: 1-800-438-6878 Website: www.mustardmuseum.com

Try the Garlic Dill Mustard or the Cranberry Mustard. Mmmmm!

MULTI-TALENTED TILAPIA SALAD
(Makes about 4 cups)

Tilapia is a nice, mild white fish that lends itself beautifully to almost any flavor you want to spice it up with. Apricot Ginger Mustard might be a little hard to find if you don't have a specialty cooking shop near you, but you can always order it from the Mustard Museum www.mustardmuseum.com. The Peanut Ginger Sauce can be found in the Oriental section of your grocery store but if all else fails, use the Honey Mustard mixed with ginger.

1 lb. tilapia fillets

2/3 C. water

1/3 C. white <u>wine</u> or chicken broth

3 cloves garlic, smashed

2 bay leaves

1 t. Herbs de Provence

1/4 C. ranch-type dressing

1/4 C. mayonnaise

1/4 C. no fat sour cream

1 t. salt

1 T. Apricot Ginger Mustard, Peanut Ginger Sauce or Honey Mustard mixed with 1/2 t. ground ginger

1/3 C. finely chopped celery

1/4 C. chopped green olives

Salt & pepper to taste

1.) Put the water, wine or chicken broth, garlic, bay leaves and a pinch of salt in a large frying pan. Add the tilapia and poach over medium heat for 10-15 minutes, depending on the thickness of the fillets. The fish is done when it is all white and flakes easily with a fork. Be careful not to overcook it. Any fish becomes tough and chewy if it is cooked too long.

2.) While the fish is poaching, whisk together the Herbs de Provence, ranch dressing, mayonnaise, sour cream, 1 t. salt and the mustard or peanut ginger sauce. Add the celery and olives.

3.) The fish should be done by now. Remove fish with a slotted spoon, shaking off excess moisture. Place in a medium-sized bowl and allow to cool for about 5 minutes.

4.) Mash the fish with a fork. This should be no problem, since you cooked the tilapia perfectly. You should be very proud of yourself.

5.) Pour the dressing/celery/olive mixture over the fish. Mix well. Chill for at least one hour.

6.) You would not believe all the things you can do with this. First of all, it makes a great sandwich, but that is only the beginning. You can stuff celery with it for a quick and easy appetizer. You can also hollow out cherry tomatoes with a teaspoon and stuff them with this yummy salad. Imagine how both of them, the celery and stuffed tomatoes...ooh, ooh and maybe some cucumber slices topped with the tilapia salad and garnished with a little fresh cilantro or fresh dill, arranged on a platter would look. Wow! You're a culinary genius. You are only limited by your imagination. Have fun!!!

****

Wine has such an extensive history, I will only be able to present a small portion of it today. Fossil vines, 60 million years old are the earliest evidence of grapes! Wine production began in Neolithic communities as far back as 8500-4000 B.C. The first proof appeared in ancient Near East and Egypt. Wild grapes never grew in early Egypt but it is thought winemaking flourished because trade had been established with Palestine and grapes were abundant there.

Winemaking scenes exist on pyramid tomb walls and large quantities of sunken wine jars were buried with the pharaohs for use in the afterlife. Archeologists theorize the jugs were buried to keep the wine cooler, therefore the ancient Egyptians must have understood how temperature effects wine. At that time only royalty and priests drank wine, the rest of the population was relegated to drinking beer.

An ancient Persian story credits a princess with the discovery of wine. After losing favor with her father, the king, she tried to poison herself by eating spoiled grapes. She got a little tipsy and fell asleep. When she awoke, she realized the things in her life that bothered her, no longer did. She became a joyful princess (probably by eating a lot of "spoiled" grapes) and once again found favor with her father. The king shared his daughter's discovery and the rest, shall we say, is history.

Wine came to Europe with the spread of Greek civilization. Both of Homer's, Iliad and The Odyssey, contain detailed descriptions of wine and its production. Hippocrates and other Greek doctors were among the first to prescribe it. Today the jury is still out on that one. Some studies say drinking a glass or two of red wine daily, has tremendous health benefits; others say it's a bunch of hooey. All I know is, occasionally, the flavor of certain foods is enhanced by a nice glass of wine. It certainly brings a lovely addition to this recipe.

SUPREMELY AROMATIC MOUSSAKA
(Makes 8-10 large servings)

I am not Greek but I love Greek food. In this recipe, I use ground turkey instead of the customary ground lamb. Please do not be freaked out by what seems like a long list of ingredients. This dish is fairly easy to prepare and your family and friends will be so impressed. All you need to serve with this is a beautiful Greek salad and a lucious white wine. Opa!

2 medium eggplants, peeled and cut into 1/2" slices

6 T. olive oil, divided	1 C. chopped onion
2 lb. ground turkey	6 cloves chopped garlic
8 oz. tomato sauce	1 15 oz. can diced tomatoes
1/2 C. dry white wine	3 T. chopped fresh parsley
1 1/2 t. salt, divided	1 t. dried <u>oregano</u>
1 t. cinnamon	1/2 t. allspice
1/4 C. pine nuts, toasted	freshly ground pepper
2 beaten eggs	¼ C. whole wheat flour
2 C. milk	3 eggs
1 T. butter, melted	1/2 C. Parmesan cheese

1.) Oil or spray 2 large cookie sheets. Arrange eggplant in a single layer on each cookie sheet. Brush the slices with 2 T. of the olive oil. Sprinkle eggplant with a tiny bit of salt. Bake at 325 degrees for 10-15 minutes. A fork should easily pierce the eggplant when it is done. Set aside.

2.) While the eggplant is baking, in a large skillet, sauté the onion in 2 T. olive oil until it is transparent and the edges are beginning to turn brown. Add the ground turkey and garlic. Cook until the turkey is brown and no longer pink.

3.) To the turkey add: tomato sauce, diced tomatoes, wine, parsley, 1 t. salt, oregano, cinnamon, allspice, pine nuts and a couple grinds of black pepper. Cook until this luscious sauce starts to bubble. Reduce heat and simmer, uncovered, for 15-20 minutes or until most of the liquid is absorbed.

4.) Cool sauce slightly, remove 1/2 c. of the meat sauce, and put it into a small bowl. Add the 2 beaten eggs slowly, stirring quickly. If the sauce is too hot and you don't stir fast, you will end up with scrambled eggs in your sauce and this is no time for that! Stir egg/sauce mixture back into the rest of the cooled sauce.

5.) Now for the white sauce. Heat the remaining 2 T. olive oil in a medium saucepan. Add flour, 1/2 t. salt and some pepper. Blend well. Whisk in the milk. Whisk until the sauce begins to thicken. Keep stirring for one or two minutes or the sauce will be lumpy.

6.) Beat the 3 remaining eggs in a bowl. This part can get a little tricky. Just relax, you already did a practice version of this with the meat sauce. So you're almost a pro. This is called tempering. Pour a very little bit of the white sauce into the eggs, while you whisk rapidly. Add a little more sauce...keep whisking. Just imagine how fabulous your upper arms will look! Gradually add the rest of the sauce, all the while whisking like mad. Stir in the butter until it is completely incorporated. Remove from the heat. The rest is easy.

7.) Spray a 13 x 9 baking pan with cooking spray. Arrange half of the eggplant on the bottom of the pan. Now add the meat mixture over the eggplant. Then add the rest of the eggplant. Pour the white sauce over all. Top with the Parmesan cheese.

8.) Bake at 325 degrees for 45 minutes. Let stand for 15 minutes before you cut into it.

9.) Now taste it. Isn't this wonderful? You should feel very proud of yourself. Three cheers for YOU!!! My 1-year old granddaughter,

Anna, loves this. Three cheers for her too!

****

The ancient Greeks and Romans had a high regard for the medicinal properties of <u>oregano</u>. At that time, oregano poultices were used on sore, achy muscles or for scorpion and spider bites. Fields of oregano covered the hillsides of Greece which is probably why the word "oregano" means "joy of the mountains."

There are many species found around the world and many times it is mistaken for marjoram...although if you learn the delicate smell of marjoram as opposed to the more pungent smell of oregano you will definitely know the difference. The plants look similar but when you smell the oregano plant you will think of pizza or spaghetti sauce.

Speaking of pizza. Before WWII, most Americans had never heard of oregano but when our soldiers discovered pizza in Italy, it wasn't long before everyone knew oregano was THE FLAVOR in the pizza sauce. A very sweet neighbor gave me a small clump of oregano for my herb garden. Since it's a hardy perennial, I have found it in my garden, in northern Illinois, as late as December. Before it gets reeeeeallly cold, I bring some in to dry. Plant some "joy of the mountains" in your own garden. Be careful...it spreads quickly.

HAWAIIAN MAHALO BURGERS
(Makes 6 burgers)

I entered this recipe in the Build a Better Burger Contest. I never heard from the sponsors. Oh well, now I get to share it with you. This burger has soooo much flavor it will bring tears to your eyes. When I cook with beef, it is ALWAYS free range, organic beef, of course you could always use ground turkey.

Burger:
1 8 oz. can sliced water chestnuts, drained
1 medium sweet onion, divided
2 lb. ground chuck or ground turkey
2/3 C. rolled oats, not quick
1 egg, slightly beaten
3 cloves garlic, crushed
2 T. liquid aminos,* or soy sauce
½ C. teriyaki sauce, your favorite
1 8 oz. can crushed pineapple, drained
1 t. finely minced ginger
Vegetable oil for grill rack
6 Kaiser rolls, split and toasted
Curry Mayonnaise, recipe follows
6 large Red Boston Lettuce leaves
Your favorite barbeque sauce

*Liquid aminos are like soy sauce but with less sodium and all the essential amino acids. You can find them at a health food store or in the health food section of some of the larger grocery stores.

Curry Mayonnaise:

1 C. good quality mayonnaise

1-2 t. curry powder, depending on your taste

1 T. honey

Whisk the mayonnaise, curry powder and honey together in a small bowl.

1.) In a food processor pulse-chop the water chestnuts and half of the sweet onion until they are finely minced.

2.) Put the minced vegetables in a large bowl. Add the ground chuck or turkey, rolled oats, egg, garlic, liquid aminos, teriyaki sauce, drained pineapple, and minced ginger.

3.) With clean hands, gently mix all the ingredients together. Blend the ingredients thoroughly but don't over mix. We want tender, juicy hamburgers here, not hockey pucks.

4.) Form into six big burgers, placing them on a large platter as you form them. Cover with plastic wrap and set aside.

5.) Now fire up your grill to a medium high heat. Put some vegetable oil on your grill rack whether you're using a charcoal or gas grill, to keep the meat from sticking. This is a good time to thinly slice the rest of your sweet onion, slice your Kaiser rolls, get the lettuce leaves ready and make the Curry Mayonnaise. It might sound like a lot to do but it's really a snap.

6.) OK ready? Put the burgers on the grill. You want a nice char on the outside while keeping the inside moist and juicy. Never smoosh the burgers while you are grilling them. My Dad used to do this. His hamburgers were always as dry as sawdust, no matter how much ketchup you dumped on them. Sorry Dad. After 5-7 minutes they'll be ready to flip. Continue grilling for another 5 minutes. Check the internal temperature with a pocket thermometer, when it reads 160-165 degrees, they're done.

7.) Remove the burgers to a large platter. While they are resting, you can toast the buns. This goes quickly so keep an eagle eye on them. Lay the buns, cut side down on the grill. Don't put them over any area of your grill that is flaming, unless of course you like charred buns. Using tongs, keep checking. You're looking for beautiful grill marks and just lightly toasted.

8.) At last you are ready to assemble your gorgeous Hawaiian Mahalo Burgers. Don't they smell great?! Spread the Curry Mayonnaise on both halves of the bun. On the bottom half, place a beautiful lettuce leaf, a burger, some sliced sweet onion and top it off with your favorite barbeque sauce. Put the lid on your burger and open wide. You'll need at least two napkins for this big, juicy burger.

One cup of pineapple is only 77 Calories. Yum! It has 35 iu of Vitamin A, 16.4 mcg of Folic Acid, 23.9 mg Vitamin C and 175 mg. of Potassium. Eating fresh pineapple helps with digestion. Next time you're grazing at a salad bar, see if there's some fresh pineapple. It will help your tummy if your eyes were too big for your stomach. Groan.

Chapter 2

Eggs & Cheese

"I'm so hungry, my stomach is doing the rhumba."

GOLDEN EGGS N' RICE
(Serves 4)

Put together a mixed green salad while this is cooking and you've got dinner. It's easy for you and your family's going to gobble it right up. This recipe is easy to double if you want to invite some friends or neighbors over.

1 C. brown rice	4 cloves garlic, crushed
2 ½ C. water	1-2 T. soy sauce or liquid
2 t. olive oil	aminos*
2 eggs, beaten	1/4 C. cheddar cheese, grated
½ C. carrot, grated	freshly ground pepper

*Liquid aminos have less sodium and contain essential amino acids. You can find a bottle of them at your health food store.

1.) Put rice, water, and olive oil in a 3 quart sauce pan. Bring water to a boil. Cover and lower heat.

2.) After 15 minutes, add the eggs, carrot, garlic and soy sauce or liquid aminos to the rice. Mix well. Do *not* add the cheese yet.

3.) When the rice is done, usually in another 30 minutes, stir in the cheese and freshly ground pepper. I discovered when you add the cheese at the end, you don't have to put in nearly as much to get that cheesy flavor.

LIFE IS NOT MEASURED BY THE NUMBER OF BREATHS WE TAKE, BUT BY THE MOMENTS THAT TAKE OUR BREATH AWAY.

Carrots are native to Afghanistan. They were cultivated in the Mediterranean area as early as 500 B.C. The Greeks called the carrot "Philtron" and used it as a love medicine. India, China and Japan cultivated it as a food crop by the 13th Century but it wasn't well-known in Europe until the 16th Century. In Elizabethan times, some people ate the carrot, while others decorated their hats and clothing with the carrots' green, feathery tops. Hmmm, carrot tops on my purple hat.

In Holland, the original carrot colors of red, purple, black, yellow and white varieties were hybridized to today's bright orange with its powerful dose of beta carotene.

Carrots arrived in America with the early colonists but were not cultivated, which changed them into the wildflower, Queen Anne's Lace. Just pull a Queen Anne's Lace up by the root and take a whiff. Hmmm....carrots.

Many who practiced folk medicine believed eating carrots lead to better night vision. This conviction enabled the British Air Force to disguise its use of radar from the Germans during World War II. The British bragged about the great accuracy of its fighter pilots at night due to being fed enormous amounts of carrots. The Germans assumed this was true because they had the same belief about carrots.

When you buy carrots in the store, remember the darker the orange color, the greater the amount of beta carotene, which converts to Vitamin A in the body. Sometimes you see carrots in the store with their tops still on. Those are picked at a younger stage and are harvested by hand instead of by a machine. Around Thanksgiving I picked up a bag of multi-colored carrots at the Trader Joe's near me. In addition to orange carrots, there were yellow and red ones. They were so sweet and fresh. Cooked or raw, they were fabulous!

One medium carrot has 35 calories, no Fat or Cholesterol, 2 g. Fiber and a whopping 270% of our required daily dose of Vitamin A...one little carrot! The latest research indicates damage to DNA (genetic material that controls cell function) leads to cancer. One of the strongest ways to protect against this damage comes from veggies, such as, sweet potatoes, brussel sprouts, broccoli and of course...carrots. In a study of women with a family history of breast cancer, those who began eating more veggies had less damage to their DNA. Do you see the good news here? These women changed a few habits and were on their way to better health. Hurray!!!

SORT OF CORN QUICHE, BUT NOT REALLY
(Serves 8-10)

2 large onions, sliced

1 C. mushrooms, sliced

3 cloves garlic, crushed

1 T. olive oil

maybe a little water or white wine

4 C. corn, frozen or fresh

2 med. tomatoes, sliced

8 eggs, beaten

3 C. milk

3 T. whole wheat flour

3 T. unbleached flour

1 T. Dijon mustard

1 t. salt

1 t. dried oregano

2 C. grated cheddar, divided

1.) Sauté the onions, mushrooms and garlic in olive oil. Sprinkle with a tiny bit of salt. Stir fry until the onions are transparent. If it gets too dry, add a little water or white wine...not too much.

2.) Stir corn into the mushroom/onion mixture. Cook just long enough for the corn to heat through. Coat the bottom and sides of a 9 x 13 baking dish with a little olive oil. Spread the vegetable mixture over the bottom of your baking dish.

3.) Now arrange the tomato slices on top of the veggies.

4.) Sprinkle half of the cheese, that's 1 C. for those of you who are falling asleep or getting distracted by telemarketers, on top of the tomatoes.

5.) It's time to prepare the custard!! Ta-da! Don't panic if you are watching your cholesterol. Egg substitutes work fine in this recipe as does low fat cheese. It's up to you, whatever makes your heart happy.

6.) OK, let's blend those eggs and the milk together. This recipe is very flexible. Beat with a whisk until they are well mixed.

7.) I'm going to tell you a little trick. Put about 1/2 C. of the egg mixture in a small jar. Add the two kinds of flour and the mustard. Put the lid on. Make sure it's on tight and shake. Do a rumba all over the kitchen.

Move that body! Work up an appetite. When you've shaken it enough, pour it back into the rest of the egg/milk mixture and you won't have any lumps.

8.) Whisk in the salt and the oregano. Stir gently till well blended. Pour it over the cheese, tomatoes and veggies.

9.) Top with remaining 1 C. of cheese. Bake at 350 degrees for 1 hour or until the top is a nice golden brown.

10.) Let stand for 5-10 minutes before cutting. Serving will be a lot easier. Add a nice tossed salad and a loaf of whole grain bread. Call everyone to the table. Dinner is served!

****

Corn is old, old, old. Fossilized corn pollen has been found in drill cores of lake sediment, beneath Mexico City, that has been thought to be 80,000 years old or more!!!! Kernels dating back to 6600 B.C. have been found in caves in Mexico. Two thousand years ago, corn cultivation spread south, as well as north, reaching into what is now the U.S. It became a staple of native tribes. In fact, corn, beans and squash were called the "three sisters," sisters who should never be planted apart.

This lip-smacking veggie played an important role in the survival of the American colonists. The type of wheat they brought over from Europe would not grow in American soil. It became vital they find another primary crop to grow. They learned to plant corn Indian-style...dig a hole with a stick then put a fish or two in the hole along with a couple kernels of corn.

Corn belongs to the grass family. The husk and cob as we know them today were gradually developed from wild varieties by native people of the Americas. As a matter of fact, the sweet corn we enjoy so much, was discovered in 1779 in an Iroquois village along the Susquehanna River in central New York. Good thing. As it was, corn's popularity as a serious food, didn't actually take off until the 1840's.

Every year, in the Midwest, during August and September, corn festivals are everywhere. Corn fritters, corn pudding, corn relishes, corn chowder, corn pancakes and a variety of cornbreads are featured items on festival menus. My favorite, though, is corn-on-the-cob. Yuuuummmmy!

Yellow corn is a good source of Vitamin A, white corn is not. One ear has 3 g. of Fiber and Protein, 416 mg. Potassium, 138 mg. Phosphorus, and is low in Fat. That is until you drown it in butter. Oh, what the heck...go ahead. There's nothing like sweet, tender corn-on-the-cob and tomatoes right out of the garden, is there? Sigh.

FIESTA BONITO BURRITO
(Serves 4)

Great for breakfast, lunch or whenever. All those fresh veggies just bursting with flavor, blended with Southwestern spices. It just makes your mouth want to sing. Ole!

2 T. olive oil
1/2 C. sweet onion, chopped
1/2 green pepper, chopped
1/2 red pepper, chopped
3/4 C. corn, fresh or frozen
1 plum tomato, chopped
3 cloves garlic, crushed
1 t. cumin

1 t. chili powder
1/2 t. oregano
Salt & pepper to taste
3 eggs beaten
4 lg. flour tortillas
2 T. fresh cilantro
1 C. cojack cheese, grated
1 avocado, peeled & sliced

1.) Sauté onion, red & green peppers, corn, and tomato in olive oil for 5 minutes, stirring frequently. Add garlic. Cook for another 5 minutes, stirring often to keep the garlic from burning.

2.) Blend in cumin, chili powder, oregano, and a little salt & pepper. Continue to cook for another couple minutes.

3.) Stir in the beaten eggs. Scramble together until egg is set and no longer shiny. Now you will have a big pile of great scrambled eggs. Put on some tango music and get ready.

4.) Preheat your oven to 300 degrees.

5.) Divide egg mixture equally among the 4 tortillas. Do the same with the cilantro, cojack cheese and avocado. Fold the bottom of each tortilla up toward the center (this is so everything doesn't fall out when you pick it up), then roll it up. You might want to secure it with a toothpick if the tortillas are trying to flop open.

6.) Place them on a cookie sheet and warm for 10 minutes. These are excellent for a fast brunch along with a fresh fruit salad. Yum-yum. When you're done, get up and do the tango.

****

<u>Cilantro</u> is another plant with a very ancient history. It has been grown in China and India for thousands of years. It is one of the few herbs which has a different name for the plant and a different name for the seeds. Versatile isn't it? The seeds of the plant are called coriander, which have a spicy, citrusy taste. The leaves are what we know as cilantro. To many people, you either love the taste of cilantro or you can't stand it. I've heard it referred to as both Chinese or Mexican parsley. I guess it depends on where you're from.

Coriander was popular in England during the Tudor Era. The Colonists brought seeds over and introduced it to America. Cilantro/coriander is very easy to grow from seed plus it self-sows . It is May in Illinois now, and my garden has a nice patch growing from seeds of lasts year's plants. This is another herb that is always in my garden. When the weather gets hot, it bolts (flowers) right away. Soon the tops will be covered with lots of little green balls. Those are the seeds. If you want to, just let them ripen, and you've got coriander, which is a great spice in sugar or oatmeal cookies. If you want your cilantro to keep going for a while, pick off the flowers. It has been my experience, once the plant produces seeds, the leafy part starts to die off, especially if it stays hot.

I love the taste of fresh cilantro. It is not an herb whose flavor is enhanced by drying. In fact, to me, compared to the fresh, it doesn't have much taste at all. The only part that should be dried, are the seeds. When the weather doesn't allow you to grow it, cilantro is available in most grocery stores all year round. Just remember, a little goes a long way. If you're just starting to cook with it, go easy. It should always be added at the end of the cooking process or used raw since it is considered to be a delicate herb. Cilantro, itself is not a medicinal herb but the seeds can be chewed to freshen the breath or made into a tea to soothe an upset stomach.

The next time you're making a tossed salad, throw in a small handful of cilantro. Every once in a while, you'll taste one of those leaves. Surprise!

BREAKFAST FRUIT PUFF
(Serves 4)

This has a lot of ingredients, but it's easy to prepare and so scrumptious.

3 T. butter
2 lg. apples, cored & cut into small chunks
1/3 C. dried, sweetened cranberries
1/4 C. brown sugar
1 t. cinnamon
1/2 t. allspice
1/2 t. ginger
1/4 t. freshly grated nutmeg

Puff part of the recipe:
2/3 C. milk
4 eggs
2/3 C. flour
2 T. honey
1/2 t. salt
1 t. vanilla
4 oz. neufchatel cheese,* at room temperature

*Neufchatel cheese is low fat cream cheese found right next to the regular cream cheese.

1.) Put milk and eggs in blender. Beat for about 20 seconds. Add flour, honey, salt and vanilla. Beat for another 20 seconds. Cut the neufchatel in chunks and put into blender. Whirl it up for about 20 more seconds. Set aside.

2.) In an oven-proof skillet, sauté apples in butter for a couple minutes. Add cranberries and brown sugar. Sauté for a couple more minutes. Next add the cinnamon, allspice, ginger and nutmeg. Sauté for one more minute.

3.) Pour the puff mixture over the fruit mixture...right in that oven-proof skillet. Isn't this easy? Bake at 375 degrees for 25-30 minutes.

Serve warmmmmm! It wouldn't hurt if you wanted to make this for dessert and serve it ala mode with an excellent vanilla ice cream.

****

Vanilla is indigenous to Central America and was first noticed by Europeans in Mexico where the Aztecs used it to flavor their chocolate drink. The vanilla vine is a member of the orchid family. Tiny hummingbirds and the Melipona bee pollinate the diminutive orchid blooms. When the vine was brought to other parts of the world, it did not produce beans until people realized the flowers could be pollinated by hand. The Totonacas people still grow vanilla vines with great devotion because they feel it is their gift from the gods.

Because the American demand for vanilla in the ice cream industry exceeded the world annual production, much of the vanilla flavoring marketed today is artificial. The artificial product is nowhere near as aromatic or flavorful as the real thing. A good friend of mine just got back from Mexico and bought me a bottle of honest-to-goodness 100% Mexican vanilla...just lovely.

Since not much was to be found concerning the nutritional value of vanilla, I thought I would give you an aromatherapy use instead. In linen closets in Veracruz, it is common to find a few vanilla beans among the bedding sheets. Vanilla scented pillow cases are said to relax the senses and make amorous hearts. Hmmm! I wonder if there is going to be a run on the sale of vanilla beans.

LOVE IS NOT BLIND...IT SEES MORE, NOT LESS. BUT BECAUSE IT SEES MORE, IT IS WILLING TO SEE LESS.

~Rabbi Julius Gordon

45

SWISS, SWISS FRITTATA
(Serves 4-6)

Swiss chard is one of my most loved vegetables. I'm so glad my favorite grocery stores carry it all year long now. I was shocked to find a lot of people cut the stems off and throw them away, I guess like you would for spinach. Surprise!!! Those stems are sweet and as wonderful as the big leafy part. This is a fast and easy way to introduce yourself to this unfamiliar green food.

8 C. packed <u>Swiss chard</u>
Excellent olive oil (you wouldn't use any other kind, right?)
1 small onion, chopped
3 cloves garlic, crushed
Sprinkle or two of salt
A couple grinds of black pepper
7 eggs, beaten (you can use egg substitute)
1 t. dried marjoram
1/8 t. nutmeg, freshly grated
1/4 C. grated parmesan
1/2 C. Swiss cheese, shredded (if you don't like Swiss cheese, you can substitute a mild cheddar, but then it will only be Swiss Frittata, not Swiss, Swiss Frittata)

Can you tell I've had a cup of coffee????

1.) Remove the stems from the chard and cut them up into one-inch pieces. Put then in a pot with a couple tablespoons of water and a tiny sprinkle of salt. Cook them gently for about 5 minutes, drain and set aside.
2.) Chop the Swiss chard leaves and sauté in your most excellent olive oil, with the onion, for about 5 minutes. You have to cook the stems

separately because they take longer to cook than the leaves.

3.) Now add the garlic, cooked stems, a smidgen of salt and a grind or two of pepper. Sauté together for a minute or so, then set aside to cool slightly.

4.) Meanwhile, in a medium-sized bowl, combine the rest of the ingredients (at this point use the salt and pepper very sparingly). Stir the veggies in to the egg and cheese mixture.

5.) Lightly coat the inside of a 9-inch pie pan with olive oil. Pour all of the egg/veggie mixture into the prepared pie pan. Bake at 350 degrees for 25-30 minutes or until the eggs are set and firm in the middle.

****

As you can tell, <u>Swiss chard</u> is the topic of conversation in this recipe. My Dad used to grow it in his prolific garden and now I grow it in mine. Chard loves the cool weather. It is one of the vegetables that you can start early in the spring when us Midwesterners are just itchin' to get back in the garden. In the last couple years, I have grown a variety called Rainbow Chard. The stems of each plant can be either red, orange, yellow or pale green. It's especially pretty in this Frittata. One year, the winter was so mild here, the Swiss chard wintered over. I still consider that one of my gardening miracles. To go out in my naked garden in February, and see this beautiful row of green, was pure joy!!!!

OK, now for the skinny on chard. Would you believe it's in the beet family and is a cruciferous vegetable? If you look at the seeds of both, you will see why. It's history goes way back to prehistoric times and was particularly prized in Pompeii! Even though it's name is "Swiss" chard, it is not native to Switzerland, it is from the Mediterranean area.

Swiss chard is so good for you, it is on Washington, D.C.'s healthiest vegetables list. In other words, it made the vegetable "A" list. One cup of cooked red or green Swiss chard has only 36 calories, 1188 iu of Vitamin A and 10.8 mg Vitamin C. It also contains lots of Iron, Magnesium, and Potassium.

This is one of the easiest vegetables to introduce to your kids. Chard doesn't leave your teeth with that squeaky feeling like spinach does (don't get me wrong, I love spinach but you know what I mean). It's much sweeter and you can hide it in a lot of things like soups, salads and casseroles. So go ahead, 'make their day.'

SALUTE TO THE SUNRISE EGGS
(Serves 4)

After you've done your yoga on the deck to greet the day, this is a good way to fire up your engine. (You'll need a 10 x 10 casserole dish for this one).

8 oz. mushrooms, sliced	6 <u>eggs</u>, beaten gently
1 small green pepper, chopped	1 scant t. sage, dried
2 T. olive oil, divided	1 scant t. salt
1 T. butter	½ t. pepper
2 T. unbleached flour	1 small tomato, chopped
1 ½ C. skim milk, divided	2/3 C. cheddar, grated

1.) In a medium-sized skillet, sauté mushrooms and green pepper in 1 T. of the olive oil for 5-7 minutes. Sometimes the mushrooms and peppers have a high moisture content. If there's a lot of liquid in the bottom of the pan, drain it off. Set the vegetables aside.

2.) Over low heat, melt the butter and the other tablespoon of olive oil in a 10 x 10 casserole dish. Stir in the flour and blend until the mixture turns a light brown. You are toasting the flour so it will have a nutty taste...not a gummy flour-y taste.

3.) Add ¾ C. of the milk. Whisk until smooth and thickened, stirring constantly...otherwise you'll have lumps. Remove from the heat.

4.) Turn on your broiler.

5.) Blend the rest of the milk, eggs, sage, salt and pepper together in a mixing bowl.

6.) Pour egg mixture into flour mixture in the casserole dish. Whisk until it's thoroughly combined.

7.) Over medium heat, move those eggs around, just like you would for scrambled eggs, until most of the liquid is gone. You'll have to stir frequently to keep them from burning. Top with sautéed veggies, chopped tomato and grated cheese.

8.) Broil 3-5 minutes until cheese is melted and has turned a nice golden brown. Piece of cake, right? Serve right away with some chilled fresh fruit. Fabulous! Now I salute YOU. Have a stupendous day!!!

****

We are not going to debate here which came first, the chicken or the egg. However, for reasons of sanity you cannot talk about eggs unless you discuss the chicken...a little. As far as my research showed me, the chicken was first domesticated in India around 2,000 B.C. and the Indians were the first to eat eggs from these tame hens.

The Chinese were the first to think of incubating eggs around 1400 B.C. Domesticated chickens reached Greece, through Central Europe, by the 5th Century B.C. Do you see how many cultures were involved in the egg movement? Wait till you see what comes next. Leif Erickson reported, when he landed in North America, "There were so many birds, that it was scarcely possible to step between their eggs." That was around 1000 A.D. So by the time Columbus got here, there were eggs everywhere. The rest is egg history.

Let's talk about egg nutrition. Three things affect the nutritional quality of the egg: 1.) what the chickens are fed, 2.) how the chickens are treated (don't laugh), and 3.) how fresh the eggs are. I prefer to buy my eggs from free range chickens. They are usually fed a better diet and are much happier chickens because they are allowed to roam around.

A friend of mine, Annie, raises about 10 or 11 chickens because she loves doing it. Her little hens are so cute. She feeds them marigolds during the summer. You should see how yellow the yolks are in those eggs. There is a big difference in the taste of a fresh egg from a happy chicken and one that comes from a chicken fed who-knows-what and never gets to see the light of day. Every once in a while, Annie has some extras and sends them over. Now that's an egg!!

Anyway, one egg generally has 79 Calories, 6 g. Protein, 260 mg. Vitamin A and 32 mg. Folic Acid. The debate still goes on about the Cholesterol in eggs... won't hurt you vs. will hurt you. This is my take on the subject. An egg is a perfect construction of the Creator. There are a lot worse things we could put in our bodies. For such a small package, an egg contains a lot of nutrition. They digest very easily as long as they aren't smothered in fat, so *go ahead*, have a couple eggs.

GREEN EGGS
(Serves 4)

I think Dr. Seuss would have loved these! I don't know if he would have missed the ham or not...I don't think so.

1 T. olive oil

1 1/2 C. sweet onion, chopped

Sprinkle of salt

1 lb. fresh baby spinach,

1/8 t. freshly grated nutmeg

1/2 C. seasoned bread crumbs

2 T. toasted wheat germ

1 T. flax seed, ground

4 eggs

Sprinkle of pepper

Sauce:

2 T. butter

3 T. flour

1 C. milk

1 C. mild cheddar, grated

1 T. honey mustard

1.) Sauté onion in olive oil. Sprinkle with salt. Continue to cook until the onion starts to turn a nice golden brown.

2.) Next add the spinach. You'll have to add the spinach a couple handfuls at a time. One pound of spinach might look like a lot but wait until you see how it cooks down. Sauté until spinach is wilted. Add nutmeg, bread crumbs, wheat germ and ground flax seed. Mix until thoroughly blended.

3.) Coat a 9 x 9 inch baking dish with cooking spray or olive oil...your choice. Spread spinach mixture in the bottom of the prepared baking dish. Make four indentations in the spinach, one for each egg...like you're making a little nest for each of them. Sprinkle lightly with pepper.

4.) Now for the sauce. Melt butter, whisk in flour. Whisk, over low flame, until well incorporated and flour mixture turns a pale golden color. Slowly add milk. Continue to whisk until mixture is nice and smooth.

Add cheese, honey mustard and a pinch of salt. Whisk until cheese has melted and sauce gets smooth again.

5.) Pour sauce over spinach and eggs. Bake at 325 degrees for 25 minutes or until the eggs are done the way you like them.

This is great for brunch with some chilled fresh mango and cinnamon bread...toasted or not. Yum, yum.

****

Spinach is believed to have originated in Persia where a wild variety was eaten. The first European plantings were thought to be taken to Spain by the Moors in the 11th century. Catherine de Medici, who married Henri II of France in 1533, is said to have loved spinach. It was introduced to her in her native Florence, Italy. Spinach seed was sent from England to America in 1787. It did not grow very well and silverbeet was used instead. Silverbeet? What the heck is silverbeet? When I first looked it up on-line I found out it was a rock group. No, that wouldn't do. Wrong silverbeet. I went to Google and found out it's what Australians call Swiss chard, which is written about in the recipe, *Swiss, Swiss Frittata*. Well anyway, I discovered Thomas Jefferson grew spinach and loved it. (I'm beginning to wonder what Thomas Jefferson *didn't* grow.)

Cooked or raw, I love spinach and have it often. It has a reputation for being loaded with iron but I found out that the oxalic acid in spinach binds up the iron and keeps most of it from being absorbed by the human body. Sorry Popeye. However, spinach is rich in lots of other good things like carotenoids, which are good for preventing macular degeneration and the formation of cataracts as we age. Vitamin A is a carotenoid. I thought you'd like to know that one C. of raw spinach contains 2014iu of Vitamin A! It's also high in Vitamin C, Folic

Acid and Fiber. Now aren't you excited about having Green Eggs today?
By the way, the National Garden Bureau declared 2002, THE YEAR
OF THE SPINACH!!! Ta-da! Way to go Spinach!

IF ONE ADVANCES CONFIDENTLY IN THE
DIRECTION OF THEIR DREAMS, AND TRIES TO LIVE
THE LIFE WHICH THEY HAVE IMAGINED, THEY WILL
MEET WITH A SUCCESS UNEXPECTED IN
COMMON DAYS.

-Henry David Thoreau

FLUFFY SCRAMBLED WRAP
(Serves 4)

If you get the chopping, grating and trimming done first, it goes together pretty fast and the results are just delicious. Have lots of napkins on hand...you're going to need them.

1 T. olive oil

1 C. onion, chopped

½ C. fresh tomato, chopped

4 eggs

1/4 C. skim milk

1 t. Herbs de Provence*

1/8 t. nutmeg, freshly grated

5 oz. baby spinach

2 cloves garlic, crushed

½ C. cojack cheese, grated

2 T. parmesan, grated

4 large flour tortillas, warmed

Salt & pepper to taste

2 T. pine nuts, toasted

1.) Over medium heat, in a large frying pan, sauté the onion in the olive oil until the onions are soft and start to caramelize. You want the rich flavor of the natural sugars in the onion to add to the vibrant taste of this recipe. Your mouth will find this blend of flavors irresistible. Don't rush this part.

2.) Add the tomato and a smidgen of salt and pepper. Sauté for another 3 minutes.

3.) In a small bowl, beat the eggs, milk, Herbs de Provence, and nutmeg together, set aside.

4.) Add the spinach and garlic to the onion/tomato mixture. Stir fry until the spinach is wilted. Add the egg mixture, stirring occasionally until they are partially set.

5.) Now toss the cheeses in. Continue cooking over a low heat until the eggs are done to your likeness and the cheeses are mostly melted. Add more salt & pepper if you want.

6.) Put 1/4 of the egg/veggie mix onto a flour tortilla. Sprinkle with some of the pine nuts. Fold one side toward the center, then roll it up. Do the same with the rest of the tortillas. Eat them immediately.

*Herbs de Provence is a blend of rosemary, marjoram, thyme, sage and sometimes lavender. You can find it in your grocery store, World Market or any fresh market store.

This makes 4 very big servings. See...wasn't that easy? The crunch of the pine nuts and the flavor of the herbs mingling with the veggies and cheese, will knock your socks off. You can eat these on the run if you want, but like I said, you'll need at least one napkin.

****

Nutmeg is one of my favorite spices. I love the smell of it freshly grated. If you have a 5-year old jar of ground nutmeg hanging around in your pantry...AGGGHHH! Throw it out immediately! Run, run to the store and buy whole nutmegs. You'll only need 4 or 5. They last longer when they're whole. Also, get yourself a nutmeg grater at K-Mart or Bed, Bath and Beyond. You will not believe the difference. That old stuff was dead...not much more than sawdust. All righty then, now that we've got that straightened out.

This fragrant spice is native to the Banda Islands of the East Indies, but has transplanted very well to Grenada in the West Indies. The inner kernel of the fruit of the nutmeg tree is nutmeg, the outer fibrous seed covering, is where the spice mace, comes from. Nutmeg is highly aromatic but bitter to the taste. A little bit goes a long way. An adventurous way to use it, is to add a little (1/8 teaspoon) to your favorite coleslaw recipe or grate some into stir-fried cabbage. It adds a wonderfully exotic flavor but is rarely used that way in the States.

Connecticut is called the "Nutmeg State." I couldn't figure out why because it isn't grown there. In my research I discovered that a lot of it was sold in Connecticut before and after the Civil War. According to Elizabeth Abbe, Librarian of the Connecticut Historical Society in Connecticut Magazine, April 1980:

"Unknowing buyers may have failed to grate nutmegs, thinking they had to be cracked like a walnut. Nutmegs are wood and bounce when struck. If southern customers did not grate them, they may well have accused the Yankees of selling useless wooden nutmegs, unaware that they wear down to a pungent powder to season pies and breads."

Weak nutmeg tea can help induce sleep. A small amount, freshly grated, has internally warming properties and will help sluggish digestion, flatulence, and diarrhea.

WARNING: Many sources said to use only small amounts of nutmeg at a time. Too much can produce dizziness or too deep a sleep, plus it's very bitter. From my sources a small amount seemed to be anywhere from 1/8-1/4 teaspoon. No more.

I keep a small jar of whole nutmeg and my nutmeg grater handy. I've been known to add a smidgen to French toast, cookies and even spaghetti sauce. Go forth now and grate nutmeg. Be creative and have fun.

CHEESY LAYERED POTATOES
(Serves 8-10)

This makes a lot but is easy to cut in half. However, the leftovers are sooooo good, you'll probably want to make the full recipe.

3 T. butter, divided
2 T. olive oil
1 C. onion, chopped
6 T. flour
1 t. salt, plus a little more
1 ½ t. Herbs de Provence

Some grinds of black pepper
1 C. half & half
2 C. milk
10 C. red potatoes, sliced
1 ½ C. cheddar cheese, grated

1.) Preheat the oven to 350 degrees. Coat a 9 x 13 glass pan with about 1 T. butter. Set aside.

2.) In a large frying pan, melt the remaining 2 T. butter with the 2 T. olive oil, over medium heat. Add the onions and sauté until they are transparent, about 5-7 minutes.

3.) Next add the flour, salt, Herbs de Provence and pepper. Whisk continuously, over low heat, until the mixture begins to turn a light golden brown.

4.) Slowly add the half & half and milk. Using the whisk, stir quickly to keep the sauce from getting lumpy. As soon as the sauce starts to thicken, remove from heat.

5.) Layer half the sliced potatoes in the prepared 9 x 13 pan. Sprinkle with a little salt and a couple more grinds of pepper. Cover the potatoes with half the sauce. Now put 1 C. of the grated cheddar on top of that.

6.) Next layer on the rest of the potato slices. Sprinkle lightly with a little more salt and a couple more grinds of pepper. Top with the remaining sauce. Save the remaining ½ C. cheese for the last 15 minutes of baking.

7.) Cover pan with foil, and bake for 45 minutes. Remove foil and bake for 15 more minutes...don't add the cheese yet. Now top with the rest of the cheese and bake for another 15 minutes. Let stand 5-7 minutes before serving.

When you bake it this way you get a nice crust on top and the potatoes are done perfectly. The leftovers are easily reheated in the oven and will "crust up" all over again. Yummy!!!

****

In this country we use mostly wheat <u>flour</u>. Flour is made from grasses like wheat, oats, rye, corn, barley and rice. It is also made from legumes and nuts, such as soy, peanuts and almonds. Flour is the key ingredient in bread and has been for thousands of years.

Originally grain was ground by hand between two stones. Grinding grain this way was a tremendous amount of work. It took several hours to grind enough grain for ONE meal. Around 6,000 B.C. sieves, made of grass, were used to sift the coarse grain from the flour. The early flours were very crude and extremely hard on human teeth.

As agriculture began to develop, wandering tribes settled and built villages. For centuries two horizontal disk-shaped stones were used to grind the grain. These large grind stones were operated by slaves, human labor or animals. Maybe that's where, "What a grind," came from. Hmmmm!

Around 25 B.C. an architect named Vitruvius invented a water mill in which a paddlewheel turned the heavy millstones by a huge gearwheel. This was used until the windmill was built in Europe around the 12th century. Development of wind or water driven mills was very expensive. The mills were usually owned by the church or royalty. Each farmer brought their grain to the local mill to be ground and would pay a fee of about 1/16th of the grain he had milled.

Early American colonists used wind power for their mills. As settlers pushed west, water-driven mills were more common. By 1878 millstones were replaced with two corrugated cylindrical steel rollers. These were much more cost effective and produced a cleaner, finer flour. Industrial mills now annually produce 320 million tons of wheat flour alone.

Whole wheat flour is made from the entire grain as opposed to bleached white flour which is whitened with oxidizing agents like acetone peroxide, benzoyl peroxide or chlorine. When wheat is stripped from the germ (where most of the nutrition is) and its bran (where the fiber is) it is then bleached and refined using up to 60 chemicals. YIKES!! I use only unbleached white flour. I've tried making chocolate chip cookies using only whole wheat flour but they turned out like small Frisbees. The general rule I use in baking is ¼ cup whole wheat flour to 2 cups unbleached white flour. That way you're getting the nutrition and fiber you need, yet the end result is something both you and your family will enjoy.

Chapter 3

Rice, Grains, and Pasta

"Mmmm...mmmm."

FORGET THE PEPPERS CASSEROLE
(Serves 6-8)

I got tired of my kids turning up their noses at stuffed peppers. They'd eat most of the stuffing but wouldn't get too close to the pepper because they "could taste it." I devised this very easy casserole so no more partially eaten green peppers would have to be thrown in the compost bin. I decided to change the format of this recipe. It's easier this way plus it felt like I was in the kitchen with you, cheering you on.

1.) Cook 1 ½ C. rice (basmati or jasmine rice would taste great) in 3 C. water and 1 t. salt over medium low heat for about 15-20 minutes.

2.) While rice is cooking, make the very easy Tomato Sauce.
    You'll need:
        28 oz. can of diced or crushed tomatoes
        2-3 cloves garlic, crushed
        2 T. chopped fresh basil or 1 1/2 t. dried
        1 t. dried oregano
        Salt and pepper to taste

Mix all theses ingredients in a medium sauce pan and simmer, uncovered for about 30 minutes, which is conveniently about the same time it takes to prepare the rest of this yummy concoction.

3.) So now your rice is cooking, maybe you'd better check it. You could probably turn it off about now and just let it steam itself the rest of the way. Just remember to keep the lid on the pan. Your sauce is getting ready to simmer...so on to the final part.

4.) Here's the rest of the ingredients:
        2 large onions, sliced

3-4 T. olive oil, divided

1 # mushrooms, sliced

1 C. mozzarella, grated

½ C. parmesan cheese, grated

5.) Sauté the onions in 2 T. of the olive oil until they are soft and starting to brown. Put in a bowl and set aside.

6.) Now do the same thing with the mushrooms using the same pan. You will probably have to add a little more olive oil. You won't need to set them aside in a bowl.

7.) Get your cheeses ready, stir the sauce and turn your oven on to 350 degrees.

8.) Now comes the fun part. Spray a 9 x 13 pan with cooking spray. Get ready to layer in the following order:

*rice first

*onions spread on top of rice

*mushrooms spread on top of onions

*sauce spread on top of mushrooms

*then sprinkle on both of the cheeses

9.) Bake, uncovered for 30 minutes. I can almost guarantee this won't make it to the compost pile.

****

Here are some of the things I found out about rice in addition to the history that is included in the Ginger Chicken Over Forbidden Rice recipe.

More than 90% of the rice consumed in the U.S. is produced in the U.S. We have 6 major rice producing states: Arkansas, California, Louisiana, Texas, Mississippi and Missouri. Those states have annual rice festivals that really sound like fun. They have rice cook-offs, craft shows, parades, frog contests, and they even crown Rice Queens. If any of you love festivals and would like to check one out, just type "rice festivals" into the search engine on your computer and see what comes up. Have fun!!!

Over one million acres of U.S. rice fields provide winter habitat for migratory waterfowl annually! Isn't that cool? Double duty. Way to go Rice Growers of America!

Rice has no Cholesterol, no Fat, no Sodium and no Gluten. It *does* have lots of Folic Acid, Phosphorus, and Potassium plus one cup only has 205 Calories (216 Calories for brown rice). White rice has .6g of Fiber, while brown rice has 3.5g. For you wild rice fans, one cup only has 166 Calories and 3g Fiber. By the way, if you want to find the calorie count of just about anything, you can go to www.thecaloriecounter.com. It lists over 40,000 foods. I compared them to other lists I have and they were all pretty much the same.

Don't you just love to learn something new every day?

ENCHANTED FOREST RISOTTO
(Serves 4-6)

Risotto has a wonderful, creamy texture and is a very simple dish to prepare. You'll need to soak the dried mushrooms in 2 cups of water for about 30 minutes before you start this. During the cooking process, risotto makes its own sauce...and the smell...well, it's simply enchanting.

1-2 oz. pkg. dried porcini mushrooms	½ C. dry white wine
4 C. vegetable broth	2 green onions, sliced
2 C. water	1 T. fresh parsley, chopped
3 T. olive oil	½ C. parmesan cheese
½ C. finely chopped onion	1 T. butter
1 ½ C. Arborio rice*	1 t. dried savory or thyme
	Salt & pepper to taste

*Arborio rice has a lot of starch that is released while you make the risotto. That's what makes true risotto so creamy without adding any cream. You can find Arborio in the rice section of your grocery store.

1.) In a medium saucepan, heat the vegetable broth and the water. Don't bring it to a boil, it just needs to be warm.

2.) Drain the mushrooms. Squeeze out most of the soaking liquid. Chop them up. It's up to you how large or small you want the pieces. I tend to favor a more rustic, chunky size.

3.) Heat the olive oil in a large skillet over medium heat. Lower the heat and sauté the onion until the edges start to turn brown. Add the chopped mushrooms, a pinch of salt and the rice. Sauté until the mushrooms start to stick to the pan.

4.) Add three ladles (I use a soup ladle) of the warm broth/water mixture.

66

Stir over a medium low heat until most of the liquid is absorbed. Risotto doesn't like to be rushed so take your time with this. Add a couple more ladles of broth. Stir frequently, adding more broth as the liquid is absorbed. Just before you add the last cup of broth, pour in the wine. When the wine is absorbed, add the last of the broth.

5.) During the last few minutes of cooking, add the green onions, parsley, cheese, butter and savory. Continue to cook until the last of the liquid is absorbed and the rice is cooked the way you like it. Smell...mmmmm. This is such an earthy dish.

6.) Serve immediately with extra parmesan cheese.

Doesn't your kitchen smell great? One of my favorite ways to eat this is with Garlic Rosemary Chicken. Talk about warm, fuzzy feelings. Better go get your slippers.

****

There are usually two kinds of <u>savories</u> grown in the American herb garden. Summer savory is an annual and has a more delicate flavor than it's cousin winter savory, which is a low-growing perennial. For the Enchanted Forest Risotto, I used winter savory. That's why I only used a little bit. I have had the same plant growing in my herb garden for 8 years. It's simple to grow and has edible light pink flowers that are a beautiful addition to salads.

Savory has been enhancing the flavor of food for over 2,000 years. According to legend, the savories belong to the satyrs...the half man, half goat creatures that inhabited the mythological forests of ancient times. The Romans used it extensively in their cooking, often flavoring vinegars with it. The poet Virgil suggested growing it near beehives because of the wonderful tasting honey it produced.

During Caesar's time, the Romans introduced both savories where they quickly became popular medicinally as well as for cooking. The early colonists brought savory to the New World as a reliable remedy for indigestion. The crushed fresh leaves can also be rubbed into insect bites for fast relief.

One of my favorite ways to use savory is to mix a teaspoon of the fresh leaves from either winter or summer savory into one cup of grated white cheddar cheese. I put a slice of fresh tomato from the garden on a piece of rye bread and sprinkle some of the savory cheese over the tomato, then pop it into the toaster oven for a few minutes until the cheese melts. Scrumptious and quick.

Next time you're in your local garden center, see if they have savory in their herb section. If they do, gently rub the leaves between your fingers. I bet at least one of the plants goes home with you and finds its way into your garden.

THE MOST IMPORTANT SINGLE INGREDIENT
IN THE FORMULA OF SUCCESS IS
KNOWING HOW TO GET ALONG
WITH PEOPLE.
-Theodore Roosevelt

ASPARAGUS AND MUSHROOMS OVER RICE
(Serves 4-6)

I always associate asparagus with spring, whether it comes gently on little kitty feet or blasting like a frustrated lion wanting to let off steam.

1 C. jasmine rice

2 lb. asparagus, trimmed and cut into 2-inch pieces

8 oz. mushrooms, sliced

1/3 C. whole wheat flour

3/4 C. vegetable broth

3/4 C. milk

1/2 C. mild cheddar, grated

4 T. olive oil, divided

1/2 t. dry tarragon

Salt & pepper to taste

2 T. parmesan cheese, grated

1.) Combine rice, 2 C. water and 1/2 t. salt in medium sized pot. Cover and cook over medium heat. When the rice is almost done, turn it off and let it steam-cook the rest of the way, with the lid on. This way it won't be sticky and clumpy.

2.) While the rice is cooking, put the asparagus in a 10" frying pan. Add ½ inch water and a little salt. Turn the heat up to medium high and put the lid on. AS SOON AS THE WATER STARTS TO BOIL, turn the heat down to low and cook it until it is tender crisp and very green. Drain and put in a bowl. Set aside.

3.) Now using the same 10" pan, sauté the mushrooms in 2 T. olive oil for 5-7 minutes. When they're done put them in the bowl with the asparagus. Add the remaining 2 T. olive oil to the pan, turn the heat down low and whisk in the flour. Cook the flour mixture for about two minutes to get rid of the raw flour taste.

4.) Quickly whisk in the vegetable broth and milk, stirring constantly until the sauce begins to thicken.

5.) Add the cheddar cheese, tarragon and the all-ready-to-go asparagus and mushrooms. Be gentle, they like to be treated tenderly.

6.) Season with salt and pepper. Serve over rice and top with the grated parmesan. This is also wonderful over pasta or baked potatoes.

You will be amazed at how much you're going to learn about <u>asparagus</u> on this one little page...maybe more than you ever wanted to know.

****

OK, as far as I could find out, it seems that asparagus is native to the Russian steppes (which are centrally located grasslands populated by nomadic people). While the ancient Greeks and Egyptians liked the wild asparagus, it seems the Romans were the first to cultivate it. Julius Caesar loved it boiled and covered in butter. Sound familiar? In fact, Roman emperors were so fond of these tender green spears, they kept special fetching boats on hand to make "asparagus runs" when the urge hit them.

During the Middle Ages it dropped out of sight, like a lot of things, then began to flourish again during the Renaissance in Tuscany, Italy. The rest is obvious. It quickly spread all over Europe and was introduced in North America by the early colonists.

Asparagus is a member of the lily family. Under ideal conditions a single spear can grow 10" in 24 hours. Talk about growing like a weed! Contrary to what some think, gourmands prefer the flavor of the thicker asparagus instead of the thin. I agree. While I do like many of my vegetables on the young, slender side...asparagus is not one of them.

According to my <u>Nutrition Almanac</u>, a 1 C. serving of asparagus contains a colossal 160mcg of Folic Acid, which is important in preventing birth abnormalities, 1202 IU of Vitamin A, and has no Fat or Cholesterol...unless, like Julius, you drown it in butter.

There is one other little fact about asparagus I thought you might be interested in. Have you ever noticed your urine has a funny smell after you've just eaten asparagus? When I was doing my research, more than one source brought up the subject of "asparagus pee." I, of course, was curious and found the smell is due to a metabolite, called methanethiol. Try dropping that little bit of info at your next party and see how astonished your friends will be at the fount of knowledge you are.

CHRIS' INTERNATIONAL PASTA
(Serves 2-3)

My son, Chris, had something like this at a restaurant he was at. Being a pasta freak, he came home and tried to duplicate it. After tweaking it a bit, this is what he came up with. We all love it...especially since it's so quick. All you need is a good green salad and you're ready to go.

1/2 lb. angel hair pasta, cooked

3 eggs, beaten

1/2 C. milk

2 T. liquid aminos or soy sauce

2 T. fresh parsley, chopped or 1 T. dried

2 cloves garlic, crushed

Freshly ground pepper

1/4 C. parmesan cheese

2 T. olive oil

1.) Cook the pasta. While you're waiting for the water to boil, you can make the rest. The pasta should be done when the rest of the recipe is finished.

2.) Beat the eggs, milk, liquid aminos or soy sauce and garlic together. Cook them, like you would scrambled eggs, in a large non-stick frying pan only break the pieces of scrambled egg into very small pieces, with a spatula, as they're cooking. They should be very dry.

3.) Add the parsley and the pasta to the pan. Toss the egg mixture and pasta together over a low heat. Turn off the heat and add freshly ground pepper to taste, the parmesan cheese and the olive oil. Toss again. Serve immediately.

This whole thing takes only fifteen minutes and is so easy to make. Have someone make the salad while you're assembling the pasta. It'll be so quick. After dinner, you might have time to catch that movie you've been wanting to see.

THE TROUBLE WITH ITALIAN FOOD IS
THAT FIVE OR SIX DAYS LATER,
YOU'RE HUNGRY AGAIN.

-George Miller

(This quote made me laugh out loud.)

Parsley is a lot more than a decoration on your plate. More than one source placed its origin in the Mediterranean area, probably somewhere around Sardinia. It was first described in a Greek herbal (a book about herbs), written in the third century B.C.

Wreaths, made partially from parsley, were given to victorious athletes in ancient Greece because they believed the god Hercules had chosen it for his own garlands. They also fed it to their horses to give them stamina to win races.

By the Middle Ages, parsley had found its way into herbal medicines especially for liver and kidney problems. It was also used for asthma, the plague, dropsy (a bacterial infection causing the stomach to bulge) and as a digestive aid.

Parsley contains more Vitamin C per volume than an orange and is high in Calcium and Iron. According to *Rodale's Herbal Encyclopedia*, doctors used to prescribe parsley tea for bladder infections.

Parsley is one of my herbal heroes. It is responsible for my serious study of herbs, medicinally. I had been using home grown herbs in cooking for about eight years before I started learning about their healing properties.

I was suffering from a bladder infection I could not get rid of. As long as I was on medication I felt OK but within three or four days of going off, the infection came raging back. My doctor kept prescribing stronger and stronger formulas. Finally, the dose was so strong, I was getting sick from the medication. I happened (I don't really believe in accidents) upon *Miracle Medicine Foods* from the 70's by Rex Adams. In the book it said to put a half bunch of parsley in a porcelain or glass bowl and pour boiling water over it. Cover and let it steep for 30 minutes then strain off the liquid and drink the "tea" throughout the day. It suggested to do this for at least three days in a row. I figured, what the heck, I was so miserable I gave it a try. I didn't feel instantly better, but on the second day I did and by the 3rd day...WOW! I was back to my old self and no side effects. I've recommended this method to a lot of people who have had equally positive results.

The next time you are in a restaurant, and see that beautiful piece of parsley resting on your plate, thank God, and eat it. At the very least, you'll have fresher breath.

UNFORGETTABLE BULGUR CASSEROLE
(Serves 6)

This dish is loaded with fiber and tastes fabulous. When I know I'm going to make this, I prepare the bulgur first thing in the morning, jump in the shower and get ready for my day. I put the prepared bulgur in the fridge where it waits patiently for me...all ready to go...when it's time to make dinner. The recipe goes together very quickly from this point.

1 1/2 C. <u>bulgur</u>

3 cloves garlic, crushed

1 C. chopped sweet peppers, vary colors

5 green onions, sliced

1 1/2 C. grated mild cheddar cheese, divided

1 15 oz. can kidney beans, drained

1 t. each, dried basil and oregano

1 ½ C. chicken or vegetable stock

Fresh pepper

½ t. salt

1/2 C. grated carrot

1 15 oz. can diced tomatoes, do not drain

2 eggs beaten

1/2 t. crushed rosemary

Salt and pepper to taste

1.) Put bulgur in a large bowl. Heat stock to boiling, pour over bulgur. Stir in garlic, ½ t. salt and a couple grinds of fresh pepper. Cover bowl with a dinner plate or large lid. Let stand for at least one hour. Go weed your garden or take a hike or prepare this in the morning like I suggested above.

2.) Add the peppers, grated carrot, green onions, diced tomatoes with their liquid and 1 C. of the cheese. Stir gently. Add the rest of the ingredients, except the remaining 1/2 C. cheese. Mix well.

3.) Place in a 2 ½ quart baking dish that has a lid...or you can use foil to cover it. Bake, covered at 325 degrees for 20 minutes. Remove lid and top with reserved cheese. Bake uncovered for 10-15 more minutes.

4.) All you need with this is a nice salad made with baby lettuces or some chilled fresh fruit...pineapple would be nice.

Call everyone to dinner. Why don't you give each of them a big hug before you all sit down? Give yourself a hug too. Love and a good meal...what else is there?

****

Bulgur might possibly be the world's first processed food. It differs from cracked wheat because bulgur has already been cooked, then dried. Making wheat into bulgur is an ancient process that originated in the Mediterranean area. It has been a key ingredient in Middle Eastern cooking for thousands of years.

Women in Syria would pound bulgur into fine particles using a mortar and pestle. This would then be mixed with onions and lamb to form a paste. The paste was shaped into a thin shell, which was then stuffed with an aromatic concoction of meat and pine nuts. This little pastry was then fried and served with yogurt and salad. I've never had one but doesn't that sound yummy? This creation is called Kibbeh and is still Syria's national dish.

In China, bulgur was decreed to be one of their five sacred crops in 2800 B.C. Many sources of archeological research have confirmed bulgur was prepared by the ancient Babylonians and Hebrews as far back as 4,000 years ago. In the Old Testament it is referred to as "arisah." The Roman word for it is "cerealis," after Ceres, goddess of the harvest.

Because bulgur resists mold and attack by insects, it can be stored for a long time, which was great for the primitive, nomadic tribes of long ago. I will just give you a note of caution here. I once bought bulgur in bulk from an open bin, stupid me. Since you're not supposed to rinse it before cooking, I cooked it and threw it into this wonderful salad I've made many times. I happened to be serving this salad at a big family party and guess what? The whole salad tasted like dirt. I don't even want to know why. Obviously we had to pitch it. So now I only buy bulgur in packages. I'm not saying not to buy it in bulk...just trust who's selling it.

Bulgur is great for you. High in Fiber, low in Fat, no Cholesterol, it even has 19g. of Protein per 1 cup serving. As an added bonus it also contains 420mg. Phosphorus and 574mg. Potassium. Way to go bulgur!!!

Find other recipes using bulgur or create your own. I love cooking with foods whose origins are from places I've never been. Good food, shared with people you love, creates some of the most unforgettable memories. Share the joy.

DESIGNER OATMEAL
(Serves 4)

What a way to start the day! This is great any time you want to be sweet to yourself and those around you. If you don't want to use butter...that's OK. Just make sure you don't use anything with partially hydrogenated oils in it.

1 C. water

1 t. salt

½ C. pecans, chopped

4 T. maple syrup, divided

1 t. cinnamon

2 t. vanilla

1 C. milk

1 C. whole <u>oats</u>, not instant

1 T. butter

2 ripe unpeeled peaches, chopped

1 T. ground flax seed

1.) Bring water, milk and salt to a low boil. While you're waiting for the milk and water to boil, toast the pecans in a frying pan, over medium heat. Stir frequently. When you begin to smell the pecans, they're almost done.

2.) Keep an eye on the milk. Don't let it boil over...that would be a big mess. When the water, milk and salt begin to boil, add the oats and reduce the heat.

3.) Try one of the pecans...careful it's hot! Is it toasty enough for you? Add the butter and stir to coat the nuts. Next add 2 T. of the maple syrup. The syrup will cling to the pecans like a long lost sweetheart. Turn off the heat and let them sit.

4.) As the oatmeal starts to thicken, add the remaining 2 T. maple syrup, peaches, cinnamon, vanilla and flax seed. Continue to cook over low heat until oatmeal is the desired thickness.

5.) Serve immediately and top with the toasted pecans. You don't need to add any sugar...just a little milk. Don't you feel like a pampered prince or princess? Not to mention, there's a lot of nutrition in this "designer oatmeal." Just don't tell the kids.

While you're eating this luscious oatmeal, ponder this for the day:

The ladder of success doesn't care who climbs it.
-Frank Tyger

When I was growing up, oatmeal was something I could take or leave. By the time I was a young married woman, "instant oatmeal" appeared. I don't mean to offend anybody but, that stuff tasted like paste. I know, because when I was making a paper mache turkey in second grade, I tried some. So I am speaking from first-hand experience here. Nowadays, instant oatmeal is much better but I still prefer the texture and flavor of REAL oatmeal...especially made the "designer" way.

The oldest known <u>oat</u> grains were found in Egypt dating from around 2000 B.C. From what I was able to find out, early oats were more of a weed. The oldest known cultivated oats were found in Switzerland. Oats were not as important to early man as wheat and barley. Some food historians believe that the oats we know today were developed in southeastern Europe, from a mutation of wild oats, just before the birth of Christ.

There are so many species and subspecies of oats, trying to identify the ancient remains of them would make your head spin. Oats were first brought, along with other grains, to North America in 1602. By 1768, George Washington had planted 580 acres of them on his farm. Have you ever seen a field of oats being touched by a gentle breeze? Ripening oats are a pale golden color. Imagine a sea of oats up against a bright blue sky. What an incredible sight! May I suggest a road trip in your near future?

Oats have been used to feed livestock, as well as people, since ancient times. In Samuel Johnson's dictionary, oats were defined as "eaten by people in Scotland, but fit only for horses in England." The Scots reply to that was, "That's why England has such fine horses and Scotland has such fine men." ha ha ha!

Today, only 5% of the oats grown are used for human consumption. I wonder if you know that part of that 5% is used in ice cream production. Yes indeedy, oat flour has long been used as a preservative in the manufacture of ice cream.

Whole grain oats are a good source of Fiber, B Vitamins, Vitamin E, Calcium, Folic Acid, Magnesium, Manganese, Phosphorus, Potassium, Zinc and many of the Amino Acids.

You know what I always say? Instead of the paste, go for the Fiber, sweetie.

Chapter 4

Veggies

"Surprise!!!"

ENERVATING EGGPLANT STACKS
(Serves 6)

This dish is not as intimidating as it looks. I have served this many times to rave reviews. I promise you, I would not make it again and again if it was one of those "fussy" recipes.

1 large eggplant
2 T. olive oil

1.) Peel eggplant and cut into slices ½ inch thick. Pick the 6 largest slices and place in a prepared 13"x 9" baking dish. Brush lightly with olive oil. Bake in a 400 degree oven for 20 minutes.

2.) While the eggplant is baking, start the filling.

Filling, first part:
Remaining eggplant, diced
½ lb. coarsely chopped mushrooms
1 T. olive oil

3.) In a large non-stick frying pan, sauté the diced eggplant and mushrooms in 1 T. olive oil until tender. Set aside to cool. Note: If it starts to stick add a little wine or vegetable broth. Don't add more oil. Eggplant absorbs oil like a sponge. Oily, soggy eggplant is not a good thing. UGH!!!

4.) If you're pressed for time, you can use your favorite jar sauce in place of the Fresh Tomato Basil Sauce recipe that follows. However, it's well worth the 20 extra minutes. Besides don't you want tell your friends and family you made this yummy dish from scratch? Or better yet, why not invite some of them over for a bite...or EVEN BETTER, invite them over and make a party out of the preparation.

After all, life is about community...isn't it?

Fresh Tomato Basil Sauce:

 1 large onion, chopped

 4 garlic cloves, crushed

 3 large fresh tomatoes, skinned and chopped or if good, fresh tomatoes
 aren't available, use a 28 oz. can of diced tomatoes, juice and all.

 1/4 C. dry red wine or 1/4 C. vegetable broth

 1/2 t. salt

 8-10 fresh basil leaves, finely chopped (or 1 t. dry)

 A couple good grinds of freshly ground pepper

 1/2 t. dried oregano

5.) Sauté onion and garlic in wine or broth. When onion is soft, add
tomatoes, salt, basil, oregano and pepper. Turn heat down. Simmer,
covered until you're ready to use it. Now wasn't that easy? And you
thought it would be hard. Pshaw!

6.) On to finish the filling. You're in the home stretch now.

To the mushroom/eggplant mixture add:

 2 slightly beaten eggs

 ½ C. grated mozzarella cheese

 ½ C. low fat cottage cheese

 ¼ C. grated parmesan cheese

 ¼ C. seasoned bread crumbs

 Salt and pepper to taste, be careful with the salt, there's
 already salt in the sauce.

Mix all of this together. Now you're ready to assemble the whole thing.
Bravo!

7.) Assembly:

*Pile the filling on top of each of the six partially baked eggplant slices which are already in the baking dish.

*Pour the tomato sauce over all.

*Top with: 1/3 C. grated parmesan, 2 T. seasoned bread crumbs, and 1/2 C. grated mozzarella cheese.

*Bake, uncovered, at 375 degrees for 30 minutes. Let stand 5 minutes before serving.

You'll love this...even if you don't like eggplant.

****

The star of this recipe is obviously eggplant. It's thought to have originated in India and was introduced into Spain by the Arabs. It was grown in Italy and England as a decorative plant because at first, the poor misunderstood eggplant was thought to cause madness. The Spaniards, however thought it was an aphrodisiac which finally made it become accepted in Northern Europe (just kidding). Some brave soul tasted it and declared it to be good or something like that.

One cup has only 22 Calories, 5g. of Carbs and 180 mg. of Potassium. Try it...I think you'll like it.

KAREN AND FRANK'S STUFFED 'SHROOM CAPS
(Serves 1-2)

Two very good friends of mine created this delicious recipe. I'm delighted they were willing to share it. It's easy and one of my favorite ways to prepare portabella mushrooms. This recipe is easily doubled so don't be afraid to make more.

2 portabella mushroom caps

Marinade:
2 T. red wine vinegar
4 T. olive oil
1/4 t. dry oregano
1/4 t. dry basil

Filling:
1 C. seasoned croutons or bread crumbs
Water
2 slices baby Swiss cheese
Salt and pepper to taste

1.) With a clean damp cloth, wipe mushroom caps thoroughly and remove stems. You can save them for stock or just toss them into your compost. Either way, they're not wasted. Pierce the caps with a fork and put them upside down in a baking dish.
2.) Combine the marinade ingredients and pour over the caps. Marinate for at least 30 minutes.
3.) Pour off marinade, leaving the mushrooms in the baking dish.

4.) Add enough water to croutons or bread crumbs to make a paste. Season with salt and pepper. Be careful with the salt, sometimes seasoned bread crumbs are salty enough. Stuff caps then top with cheese.

5.) Bake at 350 degrees for 15-20 minutes.

Love is like a mushroom. You never know if it's the real thing until it's too late.

There are over 38,000 varieties of mushrooms worldwide. Seventy-five percent of these are edible but only 2,000 of those are what you would consider appetizing. One to two percent are deadly...the rest can cause varying degrees of discomfort or extreme agony.

Mushrooms were thought to be the plant of immortality, according to ancient Egyptian hieroglyphics dating around 4,600 B.C. The flavor of mushrooms fascinated the pharaohs so much, they declared only royalty could eat them, thus assuring them the entire supply.

In many other civilizations of the world, it was believed mushrooms could produce superhuman strength and lead the soul to the realm of the gods. Later, France was the leader in the formal cultivation of mushrooms. They were grown in special caves near Paris for this unique form of agriculture.

After working out some bugs, the mushroom industry in the U.S. took off around 1914. At that time 4-5 million pounds were grown annually. The consumer paid 40-60 cents a pound. September is National Mushroom Month. Today the U.S. produces 800 million pounds of these succulent morsels annually. No wonder they have their own month.

The cap and the stem are the fleshy part of the mushroom which is considered the fruit of the mushroom, not the fungus. The fungus is underground. Isn't that interesting? Here, my whole life, I thought I was eating sautéed fungus when all the while I was eating a sort of fruit.

Portabella mushrooms are a relative of the common white mushroom and have a longer growing season . Some people, like me for instance, consider them to have an almost meat-like texture. They have almost no Fat, Sugars, or Carbohydrates. Whatever carbs they have are mostly cellulose. However, mushrooms have more protein than almost any other vegetable. One average size portabella has 2.5 grams of protein! I love all kinds of mushrooms....edible ones that is.

WOO-DEE-WOO VEGETABLES
(Serves 6-8)

Woo-dee-woo, what kind of name is woo-dee-woo you might be asking yourself. What is a woo-dee-woo? I am privileged to belong to a women's meditation group that works for world peace, the environment and the Oneness of all living things. We love each other unconditionally. Even though we are all so different, our hearts are in the same place. My husband called us the woo-dee-woos one time and the name stuck. We often refer to ourselves by that term. I made this dish for a dinner we were having and they loved it. They have all been soooo supportive through the development of this cookbook, so I named this recipe for them. Thanks, sweeties, I couldn't have done it without you. I love you.

This dish is so easy to prepare and is wonderful as a side dish with chicken or fish.

3 lb. red potatoes, cubed
2 bell peppers, seeded and cut into chunks (pick different colors to create visual interest for this dish)
2 large sweet onions, sliced
4 carrots, peeled and sliced
1 lb. mushrooms, cleaned and cut in half
2 T. butter, melted
2 T. olive oil
1 T. fresh thyme or 1 t. dry
Salt and pepper to taste

1.) Arrange vegetables in a prepared 13x9 inch baking dish.
2.) Pour the butter and olive oil over the veggies.

3.) Sprinkle with the <u>thyme</u>, salt and pepper. Now using your clean hands, mix the vegetables until they are well coated.

4.) Cover the pan with foil and bake at 350 degrees for 30 minutes. Remove the foil, stir vegetables and crank up your oven to 400 degrees. Bake uncovered for another 30 minutes, stirring occasionally, until vegetables are roasted and golden.

I mentioned above, this dish would serve 6-8, however, my husband ate half the pan one time. The smell of your house, as this is baking, will call everyone to dinner. You won't have to.

****

<u>Th</u>yme is key to the flavor of this recipe. I tried others but none seemed to be just right except thyme. It is a perennial herb that grows well, even in northern Illinois where I live. I grow three different kinds: silver, lemon and regular.

It's easy to dry and has such a wonderful flavor. I love to rub a small sprig of it between my fingers and just take a whiff. Mmm!

For those of you considering starting an herb garden, this would be one of the ones to start with. It's a good border plant because it is low growing and likes to spread out. The tiny flowers attract bees and come in pink, lavender, white and even red. I have harvested fresh thyme all winter long when we have a mild winter. So go ahead, give it a try.

Thymus was Greek for courage. The name also may be a derivative of the Greek's word "to fumigate." The herb was once burned to chase stinging insects from the house. A bed of thyme was thought to be a home for fairies. Gardeners used to set out a thyme plant for fairies like we would supply a birdhouse for birds.

It is native to the western Mediterranean area. Like a good many medicinal plants, it was brought across the Alps to monastery gardens by Benedictine monks in the 11th century. From the 15th century to the 17th century, it was used to fight the plagues that swept across Europe. As recently as World War I the essential oil served as a battlefield antiseptic. References to thyme have been made as early as 2000 B.C. in Sumerian writings.

All of my sources say it's been used for gastrointestinal complaints for years. Most commonly though, thyme tea or baths are used for those suffering from coughs, bronchitis, asthma or even whooping cough in children. When you feel a tickle or sore throat, signaling the onset of a cold, try some thyme tea to stop it in its tracks...and for heaven's sake, don't forget to put on your slippers.

SUMMER SQUASH ECSTASY
(Serves 6)

You could use a combination of roly-poly squash, which is a round zucchini, regular zucchini, patty pan squash or yellow summer squash. You might find other summer squash at your local farmers market. Don't be afraid to give something new a try. Remember, you're the chef, the choice is up to you.

A little hint: Pick squash that would be colorful. If the skins are tough, they would have to be removed so stay with young, tender squash.

8 C. summer squash, cut into 1-inch chunks
2 T. olive oil
1 C. fresh tomato, chopped
1 C. corn, cut fresh off the cob or thawed, frozen corn
2 T. fresh basil, chopped, or 1 T. dry
4 cloves garlic, sliced
Salt and pepper to taste
2-3 T. parmesan cheese

You might need a little water, white wine, or vegetable broth if the sauté starts to dry out.

1.) Heat the olive oil in a large skillet, over medium-high heat. Add the squash. Sauté quickly for about 5 minutes.
2.) Lower heat a little and add corn and tomatoes. Continue to sauté for another 3 minutes.
3.) Now add the basil, garlic, salt and pepper. Lower heat a little more. This is the point you might need to add a little liquid, depending on how much juice is in your tomato. I alternated with white wine and water,

adding just a little at a time.

4.) Cook until squash is tender. Add parmesan cheese just before serving.

This is such a quick, pretty dish and smells so heavenly while it is cooking. Serve it with grilled chicken or salmon. YUM! I hope you have a garden or a well-stocked grocery store or access to a wonderful farmers' market. I know you'll love this one.

****

Around 4,000 years ago, people started to breed animals and process their milk. Voila! Cheese was born. Cheese mostly comes from cows but also from sheep, goats, buffalo, reindeer, camels, and yaks. So if you have any yaks hanging around your backyard, you've got a great source for cheese.

Parmesan cheese was named after an area of Italy, Parma. It is one of the most popular and widely used cheeses in the world. After it is removed from the mold, it is allowed to mature for up to two years. It takes 16 liters of milk to make one kilo of cheese. Like most chilled cheeses, its flavor blooms when it is served at room temperature. If you are using grated parmesan, it is at its absolute best if it is freshly grated. Remember, a little bit goes a long way. If you use too much (which of course is relative) it can overpower the flavor of the other ingredients. I love a little bit of freshly grated parmesan on a fresh vegetable salad. Just a bit, adds a whole lot of flavor.

One ounce of hard parmesan contains 336 mg of Calcium compared to 69 mg. per tablespoon. However, one ounce of the hard cheese contains 7.32g of Fat, while the tablespoon only contains 1.5 grams. Parmesan also has slightly less Cholesterol, 19mg for one ounce of the hard and 4 mg for one tablespoon, than some its other "cheesey" brothers and sisters.

It contains 197 mg of Phosphorus per ounce which is pretty good for cheese. Phosphorus, as we all know, is essential in forming good strong bones. So go ahead, sprinkle a little parmesan on your scrambled eggs in the morning...it's good stuff.

Between all cultures and all nations, we should realize. . .
LOVE transcends all the empty space
that rests between us.

HONEY-GLAZED CARROTS
(Serves 4-6)

This is simple, simple, simple. Make some Scarlet O'Chicken and some herbed rice. Presto! Complete dinner. After dinner go soak in the tub. You deserve it.

1 lb. carrots, peeled and sliced julienne	2 T. honey
1/4 C. vegetable broth	1 T. butter
1 T. dehydrated onion	1/4-1/2 t. allspice
	pinch of salt

1.) Cook carrots in vegetable broth in a medium-sized sauté pan, with onion, stirring frequently.
2.) When carrots are tender crisp add honey, butter, allspice and salt. Continue cooking over medium heat, stirring frequently, until carrots are coated with glaze and they are done the way you like them.

We should all be concentrated on the future because we will have to spend the rest of our lives there.

Allspice is native to the New World. The earliest record of its discovery was in the West Indies in 1493. It was introduced in Europe by the Spaniards in the 16th Century. It is thought to have been used in ancient Aztec and Mayan cooking.

Allspice's name describes its flavor: clove, cinnamon, and nutmeg with a subtle pepper undertone. As with most spices, the flavor is best if you grind it from the whole berry just before you use it. You'll get a lot more bang for your buck...so to speak. If you haven't invested in an inexpensive coffee grinder that's used just for herbs, now is a good time to do that. Once you start cooking with freshness in mind and once you discover the difference in the flavor of freshly ground compared to stuff that's been sitting on your shelves for seven years, you won't go back to the "old ways."

Medicinally, allspice was used to ease rheumatic pain. Boil a small handful of the berries and make a thick paste. Place the paste in a clean, folded cloth and apply as a poultice to the affected area. Plus think how good you'll smell.

I discovered allspice relatively recently. When I want to jazz up the flavor of sautéed apples, mashed sweet potatoes or butternut squash or even roast chicken, I head for the allspice. Go on, experiment...who knows maybe it's good on scrambled eggs. Well, maybe not scrambled eggs...but then again, hmm.

CREAMY POLKA DOT POTATOES
(Serves 4-6)

3 T. olive oil

1/2 C. onion, chopped

1/2 C. red pepper, chopped*

1/2 C. green pepper, chopped

1/2 t. salt

a couple grinds of pepper

1 t. dried thyme or savory

4 T. flour

2 C. almond milk**

5 C. potatoes, peeled and thinly sliced

a smidgeon of salt

a smidgeon of pepper

2 T. raw sesame seeds

*You can use any color combination of the peppers you want or just one color, it's up to you.

**You can get almond milk at any grocery store. Use original instead of vanilla almond milk. The vanilla is sweeter, although one time we were out of regular and we did use the vanilla. Everyone loved it. Again, it's a matter of taste. You could, of course, use regular milk if you wanted to. The difference in taste is worth the adventure.

1.) Sauté the onion and peppers in the olive oil for about 5 minutes. Add salt, pepper, savory or thyme and the flour. Stir until the flour sticks to the vegetables.

2.) Slowly add the almond milk. Cook over medium heat, stirring until the sauce thickens.

3.) Using olive oil or cooking spray, prepare a 2 ½ quart casserole dish. Arrange 1/2 of the potato slices in the dish. Sprinkle lightly with salt and pepper. Cover with 1/2 the sauce.

4.) Arrange the rest of the potato slices over that. Top with the rest of the sauce.

5.) Bake at 350 degrees, covered, for 45 minutes. Remove from the oven and sprinkle with the sesame seeds. Continue to bake, uncovered, for 15 minutes.

Potato lovers and non-potato lovers gobble this right up. The red and green peppers are very jolly for a holiday dinner. You could use orange and yellow peppers for a more fiesta feel. Knock yourself out! Getting creative in the kitchen can be addicting. Watch out...you might actually get to love cooking.

****

As of this writing I have not been able to find anything about the history of almond milk. But I will tell you this. It's fabulous. For those of you who have a lactose problem, this is liquid ambrosia. Almond milk contains no animal ingredients or hormones for those of you who are concerned about that. It contains Calcium, Vitamins A & D and is an excellent source of Vitamin E. The 3 flavors I know of are: original with 7 g. of sugar per 8 ounces, vanilla with 15 g. sugar per 8 ounces, and chocolate with 20 g. sugar. They have also come out with no-sugar versions and low-sugar versions. Compare that to a lot of the fruit juices or pop you and your kids drink.

I use almond milk just like I would use regular milk in recipes. I've used it for breads, casseroles, smoothies, muffins, on cereal (I find it irresistible on oatmeal). Ice cold chocolate almond milk is heavenly. Last winter we were in the mood for cocoa but I didn't have any in the pantry. I did, however, have some chocolate almond milk. We heated it up, topped it with fresh whipped cream and a dash of cinnamon...well...sigh.

It has no Cholesterol, only 1% Fat, and is very low in Sodium. No, I do not get a kickback from any company if I endorse the stuff. I just happen to like it...a lot, and am always in the market for new products that are good for the body and taste good.

THE WORLD LOOKS BRIGHTER FROM BEHIND A SMILE!

POTATO BUTTERNUT MASH
(Serves 6-8)

I'm not really a mashed potato freak, but I *really* like them this way.

4 C. butternut squash, peeled and cut into chunks

2 C. potatoes, peeled and cut into chunks

8 cloves garlic

1-2 T. butter

2 oz. cojack cheese, grated

1 t. cumin

2 T. sesame seeds

Salt and pepper to taste

1.) Boil squash, potatoes and garlic in 1/2 C. water. Add 1/2 t. salt. Cook until tender.

2.) While the potatoes and squash are cooking, put the cumin and sesame seeds in a small frying pan. Over medium low heat, toast them, stirring constantly. This should take about 5 minutes. Set aside.

3.) Drain most of the water out of the potatoes and squash. Mash to the desired consistency. Stir in butter and cheese.

4.) Season to taste with salt and pepper. Stir in toasted sesame seeds and cumin.

I swear...you are going to love this. This is a great way for your kids to eat squash. They will never know what hit them.

RAISING CHILDREN IS LIKE BAKING BREAD, IT HAS TO BE A SLOW PROCESS OR YOU END UP WITH AN OVERDONE CRUST AND AN UNDERDONE INTERIOR.

-Marcelene Cox

Butternut squash is considered one of the New World foods, meaning it's very old. Europeans didn't even know about squash or beans or corn until they were introduced to them by their countries' explorers. Squash is native to North and South America. Butternut squash, a winter squash like acorn or spaghetti squash, probably originated in northern Argentina near the Andes. Winter squash have a much harder skin unlike their summer squash cousins, zucchini or yellow crookneck squash. Winter squash are still not well known in Europe because they like a long, hot growing season with not too much rain, unlike Europe's cooler wetter summers.

This is such a great squash and pretty easy to grow. The second year I planted it in my garden, I got it in late but my three vines still produced about 50 lbs. of the prettiest butternut squash you ever saw. This year, I've promised myself to get it in a lot earlier.

Butternut is really high in Vitamins A & C, which are both antioxidants. In fact, 1 cup contains 8610 iu of A!!! It has no Cholesterol or Fat and also has a high level of Potassium. When you go to the grocery store to pick one out, choose one that is heavy for its size and does not have a shiny, tender rind. Pick one with no brown spots and a smooth skin. Then go home and make this recipe.

EGGS-TERRESTRIAL EGGPLANT
(Serves 2-4)

Your kids will think it is out of this world. tee hee I couldn't resist. Anyway, one year I had so many eggplant in my garden, I had to invent ways to use it up quickly. With the bread crumb and cheese topping, this was a very scrumptious way to get kids to eat a vegetable they're not sure they'll like. Two eggplants might sound like a lot but they are mostly water and will cook down to a much smaller amount than when you started.

2 medium eggplant, peeled
and cubed
8-10 cloves garlic
1/3 C. water
1 egg, slightly beaten

1 T. butter
1 t. marjoram
Salt and pepper to taste
1/4 C. bread crumbs*
3 oz. jack cheese, grated

*This is a good way to use up bread that is getting old. Just put it in a food processor and whirl away. Of course you can always use store bought crumbs...whatever you have lying around.

1.) Put eggplant, garlic and water in large saucepan. Cook over medium low heat until eggplant is tender. Drain, leaving a little of the cooking liquid in the pan.
2.) Mash eggplant and garlic. Stir in beaten egg, butter, marjoram, salt and pepper. Turn into prepared 1 qt. baking dish.
3.) Top eggplant mixture with cheese and then bread crumbs..
4.) Bake in 350 degree oven for 20-25 minutes, until bread crumbs are real toasty and cheese is melted. Easy huh?

If you have any leftovers, this makes a great sandwich spread. Just spread it on a flour tortilla or slice of bread, top with a couple slices of tomato...instant lunch. You can also add a little more cheese or not, warm it up or not, and use it as a dip with pita or bagel chips. Get creative. I stirred a little mayo in the leftovers once and made stuffed celery when I needed a little snack-y thing for unexpected company. They loved it.

****

Marjoram was called "joy of the mountains" by the Greeks. Young Greek couples were crowned with it at their weddings. Legend said that if you anointed yourself with marjoram before you went to sleep, you would dream of your future spouse. It was once the herb that signified marital bliss, now it is more likely to be identified with turkey stuffing.

Soaking in a warm tub of marjoram tea not only scents the body but relieves aches and pains and chest congestion. Long ago it was used to help against asthma, indigestion, rheumatism, toothache, and conjunctivitis.

I absolutely love the fragrance of this herb. I will never have an herb garden without it. I always have a big pot of it on my deck. Many mornings, whether I'm using it at that time or not, I will gently rub it between my hands just to release some of its fragrance. My Dad always used it in the scrambled eggs he made for all of us on Saturday mornings. It is actually the first herb I was introduced to. Obviously, by association, I consider this a very cozy herb.

IF YOU TAKE CARE OF THE MOMENTS, THE YEARS WILL TAKE CARE OF THEMSELVES.

EXPRESS VEGGIES OVER CRUNCHY POTATOES
(Serves 4)

Your oven does most of the work for this one. Start at 4 pm and dinner will be ready by 6. This is very easy for those nights when you're either too tired to cook or you just plain don't feel like it. Throw a salad together and you're all set.

4 large baking potatoes

2-3 T. olive oil

2 C. broccoli flowerets

1 medium onion, sliced

1 small eggplant, peeled & cubed

1 medium zucchini, sliced

3 cloves garlic, crushed

1 can cream of mushroom soup

1/2 C. milk

1/2 C. low fat sour cream

Salt & pepper to taste

1.) Pierce potatoes a couple times with a fork and bake for 2 hours at 375 degrees. I think it was the famous James Beard who used to bake potatoes this long. The outside is crunchy, which I love, and the inside is moist and fluffy. YUM! If you don't pierce them, they will explode in your oven. UGH!!! What a mess. While the potatoes are baking you could go take a bath, go for a walk, play with your kids, or read that magazine you've been meaning to get to.

2.) When the potatoes have been in the oven for about an hour and a half, you can start the sauce. In a large frying pan, sauté the broccoli, and onion in the olive oil. Sauté for about five minutes.

3.) Now add the eggplant, zucchini, and garlic. Continue to sauté for another 10 minutes. When the vegetables are done the way you like them, add the mushroom soup. I know this is a processed ingredient. You won't see too many in this book (in fact this might be the only one), but every once in a while, I take a short cut.

4.) Slowly stir in the milk. When the sauce starts to bubble, turn the heat down to low and add the sour cream. Stir slowly until the sour cream is completely incorporated and barely warm. Don't cook the sour cream too long or it will break (then it looks sort of cottage cheese-y). Taste it. Does it need a little salt? a little pepper? Add what you want until it's just the way you like it.

5.) By now the baked potatoes will be done. You're ready to serve. Split the baked potatoes. You won't need any butter. Just spoon the sauce over the top and dig in. This is a great way to eat baked potatoes and get those veggies in too.

****

Broccoli is known as the "Crown Jewel" of nutrition. It was a favorite of Romans 2,000 years ago and they didn't even know how good it was for them. During the 16th century it was grown in France and Italy. The word broccoli comes from the Italian word, "brocco" meaning arm branch. Americans have sporadically grown it for 200 years or so, but most had never heard about this noble vegetable until 1920, when the first commercially grown broccoli was harvested in Brooklyn, New York.

When my husband and I were driving, west of Phoenix, we saw a beautiful sight...broccoli! There, with desert all around, was a magnificent emerald field of broccoli. Over 30,000 plants can grow in one acre of land. A field can be harvested 2 or 3 times before all the broccoli is removed. In the last 25 years, the consumption of this tasty vegetable has increased 940%!!!!

Here's a good reason why. Besides tasting yummy, broccoli has as much Calcium per ounce as milk. It contains phytochemicals which prevent carcinogens (cancer causing substances) from forming. Phytos are little agents that help boost enzymes that detoxify carcinogens. One cup of raw broccoli is only 24 Calories, has 1356 IU of Vitamin A, 62 mcg of Folic Acid, 82 mg of Vitamin C, 22 mg of Magnesium, 58 mg of Phosphorus and 286 mg of Potassium! Talk about a powerhouse! Broccoli is really one of the good guys.

FOOD IS AN IMPORTANT PART OF A BALANCED DIET.

-Fran Lebowitz

RAINBOW STIR FRY
(Serves 4)

I luuuuv this dish. I always feel so blessed when I make it. The variety and the color of the vegetables makes me so happy. All of these veggies are easy to find. A farmers market is a great place to start but what's really great, is all of these are available all year round, so you can have a rainbow on your plate whenever you want.

2 T. olive oil

4 C. purple cabbage, shredded

2 T. olive oil

1 1/2 C. julienned baby carrots

1 lg. onion, sliced thin

1 sweet red pepper, sliced into thin strips

1 C. corn, fresh or frozen

2 C. zucchini, sliced

1 1/2 C. mushrooms, sliced

3 cloves garlic, crushed

1 med. tomato, chopped

1 t. dried marjoram

1.) Prepare all your vegetables first. It's a lot easier on you when you do.

2.) You'll need two frying pans. The purple cabbage has to be cooked separately because the color will "bleed" into the other vegetables. It's not a pretty sight. Start stir frying the cabbage in the olive oil in one pan. It'll take fifteen minutes over medium heat.

3.) In the other pan, stir fry the carrots, onion, and red pepper in the additional 2 T. olive oil. This is not as tricky as it sounds, even if you are doing it by yourself. Sauté for about 10 minutes over medium heat.

4.) Lower heat and add corn, zucchini, mushrooms and garlic.. Sauté for five more minutes.

5.) Throw in the tomato and the marjoram. Cook for a couple minutes. The cabbage should be done by now. Isn't it nice how this all comes together?

6.) On a platter, arrange the purple cabbage making a nest around the edge. Put the rest of the vegetables in the center. Now isn't that pretty? This can be used as a side dish, a topping for baked potatoes, or over pasta or rice. If you're using it for a main course, you might want to top it with some cheese. You decide. After all, you're the chef.

****

Purple cabbage is obviously related to it's more familiar cousin...green cabbage. Cabbage is one of the world's most popular vegetables. Its origin is ancient. Aristotle followed the Egyptian custom of eating cabbage before banquets to prevent inebriation. Cato, an ancient Roman statesman, considered it a remedy for ailments from sore throats to cataracts.

The European aristocracy, in the 14th ~17th centuries considered cabbage to be too common for their palates, but it was one of the staples of the peasant diet. On the whole, vegetables, particularly leafy ones, were frowned upon and thought to be responsible for ill health. It truly was the Dark Ages.

In ancient China, to the present, cabbage leaves were dried, then stored for the winter. Then they would be rehydrated and used in soups and stir fries. The Chinese and Russian peasants used pickled cabbage often as an accompaniment to their meals.

Cabbage is in the cruciferous vegetable family which also includes broccoli, Brussels sprouts, cauliflower, kale and collards. Research has discovered that vegetables from this family inhibit the growth of breast, stomach and colon cancer due to the phytochemicals called indoles. Indoles tend to burn up the female hormone, estrogen and can ward off cell changes that lead to colon cancer. Some of the phytochemicals even seem to produce anticancer enzymes. However, consuming large amounts of cabbage may lead to thyroid problems. A well known remedy for healing peptic ulcers is drinking cabbage juice due to the Vitamin U it contains.

Purple cabbage is higher in Fiber, Vitamin C, Iron, Calcium and Potassium than its green cousin. When you're making your favorite coleslaw recipe, use half green and half purple cabbage. Throw in some grated carrots and toasted walnuts.

Mmmmmm! Very pretty and good for you too.

HEAVENLY GREEN BEANS
(Serves 4)

Green beans straight from the garden are one of my favorite summer treats. My Dad used to grow both green and yellow ones. My husband likes to grow purple beans to surprise the kids. When you cook them, they turn green. They taste exactly like regular green beans whether you eat them raw or cooked. This recipe makes the most of the flavor of beans no matter what time of year you eat them or what color they are.

1 lb. <u>green beans</u>, as thin as you can find them	1 large tomato, cubed
1 medium onion, sliced	2 T. fresh basil
2 T. olive oil	¼ C. Romano cheese, freshly grated
7 cloves of garlic, peeled and sliced	½ t. seasoned salt
	freshly ground pepper

1.) Steam <u>beans</u> for 5-7 minutes, depending on how thin they are. Run under cool water to stop the cooking process. Set aside.

2.) In a large skillet, over medium heat, sauté the onion in olive oil until caramelized. This step takes about 15 minutes.

3.) Lower the heat and add the garlic. Be careful, you must stir constantly or you'll burn the garlic. Garlic is very bitter when it's burned. This only takes a minute.

4.) Add cubed tomato. Cut the basil into slivers and throw that in too. Cook, stirring occasionally for about 5 minutes. Now add the cooked green beans, Romano cheese, salt and pepper. Stirring gently, continue until the flavors are well blended and the beans are warmed thoroughly...2-3 minutes at the most.

You are going to LOVE these. If you keep nibbling at them, there won't be any to put on the table.

A NICKEL (THIS IS OBVIOUSLY A VERY OLD QUOTE) WILL GET YOU ON THE SUBWAY, BUT GARLIC WILL GET YOU A SEAT.
-Old New York Saying

As of this writing, I cannot find anything about the history of the <u>green bean</u>, but I have found extensive information on how to plant them. Maybe that will be part of another cookbook. I did find information on what a green bean really is and I was surprised. I love being surprised. Well, here it is...GREEN BEANS ARE SIMPLY THE UNRIPE PODS OF DIFFERENT TYPES OF KIDNEY BEANS!!! I never knew that. So if you don't pick the beans soon enough, just let them hang on a little longer and you will have an altogether different type of bean.

Green beans used to be called string beans because of the long, fibrous string in them but that has been bred out. Now they are called snap beans. Green beans have much less Protein than their dried bean counterparts. They do have a lot of Vitamin A and about 230mg. of Potassium per cup. When you're preparing them, the less cuts you make in them, the more tender they are.

The French like to pick their green beans when they are not much thicker than a nail. They use very little water when they cook them, turn the heat up high, and wait for the water to boil. As soon as it does, they turn the heat down to very low, then add some butter, salt and a squirt of fresh lemon juice.

The beans are only cooked for a couple more minutes from that point. Voila! Perfectly cooked snap beans. Try them...they're pretty addictive. A little fresh thyme or marjoram thrown in during the cooking process, also adds a wonderful flavor.

IT'S BIZZARE THAT THE PRODUCE MANAGER IS MORE IMPORTANT TO MY CHILDREN'S HEALTH THAN THE PEDIATRICIAN.

-Meryl Streep

PEEK-A-BOO CAULIFLOWER
(Serves 4-6)

This is a recipe that needs some attention for about 30 minutes. It goes well with something that you can throw in the oven like a roast chicken or a nice, thick piece of salmon. Then you can forget about what's in the oven and concentrate on the cauliflower. You will need a 12" skillet with a lid.

1 medium <u>cauliflower</u>, broken into flowerets

¾ C. flour

¼ C. seasoned bread crumbs

2 T. parmesan cheese, divided

½ t. seasoned salt

1-2 t. curry powder

a couple grinds fresh pepper

3 T. olive oil

10 cloves garlic, crushed

1.) Put <u>cauliflower</u> flowerets in a colander and run under cold water, making sure all the flowerets get wet. Shake to drain off any excess water.

2.) In a large plastic food storage bag, put the flour, bread crumbs, 1 T. parmesan cheese, salt, curry powder, and pepper. Close bag and shake well to mix ingredients.

3.) Next put the cauliflower in the bag, close and shake well, making sure each piece is well coated with the crumb mixture.

4.) Heat the olive oil in a large frying pan. Put cauliflower in the hot oil and stir fry over medium heat, until most of the oil is absorbed. As the cauliflower starts to turn brown, add the garlic. Stir for a minute or two being careful not to let the garlic burn. Now comes the peek-a-boo part.

5.) Add 3 T. water, lower heat and put lid on pan (if you don't have a lid, a heavy piece of foil will work). Check periodically (peek-a-boo) until the water is gone. Keep adding water, 3 T. at a time, stirring occasionally, until cauliflower is tender.

6.) I have to add water five or six times. It depends on the size of the flowerets, how many times you have to add water. Smaller pieces get done quicker.

7.) When the cauliflower is tender, continue to cook until all liquid is absorbed and the light, brown color gets a little deeper. Just before serving sprinkle another tablespoon of parmesan on top.

CAUTION: Do not add water all at once! It washes the coating off and you have a big mess. If you do it the peek-a-boo way, the coating makes its own sauce that completely covers each piece.

People who don't like cauliflower, wrestle for these leftovers.

****

Cauliflower originated over 2,000 years ago in the gardens of Asia Minor and the Mediterranean area. By the 16th Century, it was eaten throughout Western Europe. It is considered, "Queen of the Cabbage Clan." Mark Twain dubbed it, "cabbage with a college education."

The name means cabbage flower because it really is a flower. As the cauliflower plant grows, a flower bud forms in the center of the plant. That bud is a baby cauliflower. Growers fold the outer leaves of the plant over this bud to give cauliflower its creamy, white color. If the bud gets too much sunshine, it turns yellow. When I was a "budding" gardener, I grew it one summer, that is I tried to grow it. The outer leaves kept sneaking out of the rubber bands. I grew yellow cauliflower, but we ate it anyway. It didn't taste as yummy as I thought it should but I don't know if that's because it didn't look like I thought it should. A couple months ago, while I was grocery shopping, there were yellow, green, purple and white cauliflower all mixed together in one happy pile. Who knew?

John Hopkins University in Baltimore, did a study on cauliflower. They discovered that this educated vegetable contains sulforaphane which lowers estrogen levels which lowers the chances of breast and prostate tumors. Also cauliflower is high in Vitamin C and Folic Acid both of which help build the immune system. Folic Acid helps blood work more efficiently. Three flowerets provide 67% of your daily Vitamin C requirements.

An easy way to get more into your diet is to lightly steam it, marinate it overnight in your favorite Italian salad dressing and just have it as a snack. I also love it raw with a good bleu cheese dressing or maybe homemade ranch dressing or hmmmm! what about creamy garlic dressing. Yum! Excuse me while I see if I've got any cauliflower in the fridge.

WONDER BEANS
(Serves 4)

Don't you just love tender green beans fresh from the garden or farmers market? You could use yellow beans if you'd like a change or some of both if you'd really like to "mix" it up. Hahahaha. In the summer I make this all the time. When you want to make it during the winter and you can't find good fresh beans, you can use frozen whole beans instead.

1 1/4 lb. fresh green beans	2 cloves garlic, crushed
2 T. olive oil	1-2 T. liquid aminos or soy sauce
½ C. onion, finely chopped	1-2 T. peanut sauce*

*You can get peanut sauce in the Oriental section of your grocery store.

1.) Using a large frying pan with a lid, cook beans, covered over medium heat, for 5 minutes in 2 T. of water.

2.) When the beans are tender crisp, rinse under cold water, drain and set aside.

3.) Heat olive oil in pan. Sauté onion until it starts to turn brown. Add garlic and sauté for a couple more minutes.

4.) Return beans to the pan. Add liquid aminos or soy sauce and peanut sauce. Stir over medium low heat until beans are well coated. Peanut sauce can be very spicy, depending on the brand. How much heat do you want? Add a little at a time until you get it the way you like it. DO NOT OVERCOOK THOSE BEANS!!!!

This goes very fast and is fabulous with grilled salmon, roast chicken, or some grilled shrimp. Mmm...mmm. Pass me the peanut sauce.

COOKING IS LIKE LOVE. IT SHOULD BE ENTERED INTO WITH ABANDON OR NOT AT ALL.

-Harriet Van Horne

<u>Onions, onions, onions</u>...what a versatile vegetable. Many times I have to search and search for the tiniest bit of information on a particular food. This was not the case with the onion. I could have written a whole book on the onion alone. Shakespeare mentions them, songs and poems have been written about them and there was more history concerning onions than I have seen for any other food...except potatoes.

This is one of those foods whose cultivation is older than history. Some sources believe onions originated in central Asia or the Mediterranean 5,000 years ago. The National Onion Association says they were probably first grown in Iran and Pakistan. Egyptians left them in their tombs 3,500 years ago. In fact, the mummified remain of King Ramses IV, who died in 1160 B.C., had small onions in the eye sockets. Archaeologists think they had some spiritual significance plus the small ones replicated a real eyeball. Paintings of them appear on some of the inner wall of pyramids in both the Old and New Kingdoms of the Egyptian upper classes.

Evidence shows Sumerians growing onions as early as 2,500 B.C. They are mentioned in the Biblical book, Numbers, and archaeologists found cavities in the gardens where the bulbs had grown in the city of Pompeii. Texts from India, dating back to the 6th Century talk of their medicinal use. Evidently they were used as a diuretic and to promote healthy hearts, eyes, and joints.

More recently, an early 1900 seed catalog offered red, yellow, white, oblong,

117

globe and spindle-shaped onions. In 1945, analysis of their sulfur compounds (the compound that makes people cry while cutting them) resulted in breeders being able to develop a sweet onion.

Onions have no Fat or Cholesterol, and are low in Sodium. Recent studies are being done on their benefit to the heart and the immune system. 1/2 C. contains 9.6mcg of Selenium and 248mg. of Potassium.

The pessimist reminds us that the lily belongs to the onion family, while the optimist reminds us that the onion belongs to the lily family.

(It's all a matter of perception. Hmmm, is this a light bulb moment?)

PRACTICALLY PERFECT POTATO PANCAKES
(Serves 4)

Talk about comfort food. This is an updated version of my Grandma Elsie's potato pancakes. I love these on a cold, wintry day with a nice dollop of homemade cinnamon applesauce. They are soooo easy to make, especially if you grate the onions and potatoes in the food processor. I like to make mine in my Grandma's cast iron skillet, like she did. Grandma used to serve them with a side of bacon...that's up to you. This is not just for breakfast. It's great for dinner too.

4 C. grated, unpeeled <u>potatoes</u>	scant teaspoon salt
1/2 C. onion, grated	2 cloves garlic, crushed
3/4 C. flour	Safflower oil
1/4 C. wheat germ	Apple sauce
2 eggs, beaten	Sour cream, optional

1.) Mix all the ingredients together except the oil, the applesauce and the sour cream. Heat your oven to 250 degrees.

2.) Warm up your skillet or frying pan first, before you add the oil. You won't need as much this way. Put a little oil in the pan and swirl it around so the bottom of the pan is coated. Put a heaping tablespoon of the <u>potato</u> mixture in the pan and flatten it out with the back of the spoon. You should be able to cook 3 or 4 pancakes at a time, depending on their size.

3.) Let them fry for a couple minutes. Lift them up with a spatula to check for browning. Some people like them very light, others like them crispier. What is your preference? When they're done they way you like them, flip them over. Continue cooking until both sides are browned. Drain on paper towel.

119

4.) Line a cookie sheet with a double layer of paper towel. Put the cooked potato pancakes on the cookie sheet and put them in the oven to keep them warm.

5.) Finish making the rest of the pancakes, putting a little more oil in the pan to keep them from sticking. Each time you get some done, stick them in the oven with the others to keep them all warm and toasty. This way, your whole family, including you, can sit down and enjoy them together.

****

Potatoes are another ancient vegetable. They are indigenous to the Andes in South America. Native Americans have been cultivating them since at least 3,000 B.C. Now comes some very interesting information. You will see how this common vegetable fed a civilization, decimated a civilization and influenced a Presidential election.

When explorers first found the Peruvian Indians they were drying potatoes in the sun. Dried, they were easy to store, could be pounded into flour, or reconstituted whole. Along with maize, potatoes were the mainstay of the Incan civilization.

In 1847-48 a terrible famine hit Ireland due to the failure of the potato crop. The Irish had become very dependent on the potato, which had been introduced in Ireland around 1565. Starvation caused the deaths of 1,500,000 people. Another million emigrated, mostly to America. There, most of them found menial labor just to survive.

Along comes the famous Lincoln-Douglas debates. Lincoln was considered the least likely to win. Douglas often made cruel remarks about Lincoln's background of poverty. When the new Irish American citizens heard what Douglas had to say about Lincoln, they supported the underdog...Lincoln. The Irish vote was a deciding factor in Lincoln becoming President. All because of a shortage of potatoes.

Almost everyone I know loves potatoes. A friend of mine introduced me to baked red potatoes. I'd never had one before. She baked them, put a little butter on them, piled on some crab meat and topped them with cheese. Yowsa!

One medium size baked potato has 2.4 g. Fiber, 19.2 mcg. Folic Acid, 30 mg. Vitamin C, 80 mg. Phosphorus, and a whopping 611 mg. Potassium. Talk about nutrition packed in a small package!

Part of the secret of a successful life
is to eat what you like
and let the food
fight it out inside.

-Mark Twain

Chapter 5

Sandwiches

"Could it get any hotter?"

GRILLED VEGGIE SALAD SANDWICHES
(Serves 4)

This is a very fast sandwich if you have a salad shooter or a food processor. If you don't have either of these, think of the muscles you're building while you're grating your veggies by hand.

1/2 C. zucchini, grated

1/2 C. carrot, grated

1/4 # mushrooms, finely chopped

1/4 C. onion, finely chopped

1 C. Chihuahua cheese, grated

1/2 c. mayonnaise

1/2 C. sour cream

1 t. dry tarragon

Salt & pepper to taste

Butter, softened

8 slices of excellent bread

2 medium tomatoes, sliced

1.) Mix veggies, cheese, mayonnaise, sour cream, tarragon, salt and pepper together. It looks very salad-y at this point.

2.) Lightly butter one side of the 8 slices of bread.

3.) Put 2 tomato slices on the unbuttered side of 4 of the slices of bread.

4.) Pile the veggie/cheese mixture on the tomatoes and top with the remaining slices of bread, butter side out. Got it? Bread...tomatoes...veggie mixture...bread. Good job! Now fire up your non-stick frying pan.

5.) Grill each sandwich over low heat so the cheese has time to melt and the veggies are cooked ever so slightly. Doesn't this smell fabulous?

SERVE IMMEDIATELY

IT'S DIFFICULT TO THINK ANYTHING UNPLEASANT WHILE EATING A HOMEGROWN TOMATO.

-Louis Grizzard

Zucchini is such a versatile vegetable. It can be easily combined with lots of different veggies and still hold its own. In my research one source said it originated in South Africa, another said archaeologists traced its origins back to Mexico dating back from 7,000 to 5,500 B.C. Either way, it is part of what has been referred to as the "three sisters" in the ancient pre-Columbian diet consisting of maize (corn), beans and squashes.

When early explorers brought it back to Italy, it was named zucchino. The New England colonists adopted the name squash from several Native American words meaning "something eaten raw." Thomas Jefferson and George Washington were big fans of zucchini.

Mexican and European markets sell bunches of zucchini flowers as food. Fried squash blossoms with an orange marmalade dipping sauce are out of this world. You can also stuff them with an herb cream cheese and lightly fry them. Squash blossoms can be an unusual appetizer that adds an adventurous note to your next dinner party.

If you've ever grown zucchini, you know that if you don't check the plants every couple days, you're likely to end up with a zucchini torpedo. I've grown them for years and am still amazed at how quickly they grow...especially after a good rain.

By the end of summer, I'm looking for all kinds of new ways to make it. I love using the big ones to make Zucchini Parmesan. Just take any good Eggplant Parmesan recipe and substitute zucchini. Even my kids like that one. They think it tastes like pizza.

1/2 C. of zucchini is only 13 Calories because it's 95% water! It has lots of Antioxidants, Beta Carotene and Potassium. Be adventurous...try it...you'll like it.

ISHY'S SQUISHY SANDWICHES
(Serves 4)

You'll need plenty of napkins with this one. In fact, this sandwich would be perfect for a picnic. This recipe makes four large sandwiches.

4 very fresh 6" sub rolls
1 large eggplant, peeled and sliced lengthwise, in ½" planks
1 C. julienne-cut carrots
1 C. sliced mushrooms
1 C. red pepper, cut in strips
1 C. zucchini, sliced

2 cloves garlic, pressed
Olive oil
2 t. fresh marjoram
Salt & pepper to taste
2 large tomatoes, sliced
1 C. grated mozzarella

Homemade buttermilk salad dressing, the kind you can make from packets in the grocery store

1.) Since eggplant absorbs oil like a sponge, we're going to be cooking it separately. Spray a couple cookie sheets with some cooking spray. Arrange the eggplant on the cookie sheets. Brush eggplant lightly with olive oil. Bake at 350 degrees for 15-20 minutes, until soft. Remove from oven and set aside.

2.) While the eggplant is baking, sauté the carrots, mushrooms, red pepper, zucchini and garlic in olive oil, until they are cooked the way you like them.

3.) During the last few minutes of sautéing, season with marjoram, salt and pepper.

4.) Now for the assembly. Slice the rolls lengthwise and spread each side generously with some of the buttermilk dressing. Then put down a slab of eggplant, next some of the sautéed veggies, followed by a couple tomato slices and ending with some cheese.

5.) The trick is to do this while the vegetables are still warm so you can melt the cheese with just the heat from the veggies. You can help the process along by wrapping each assembled sandwich in a clean dish towel for a few minutes.

This technique creates a little "steam room" for all the ingredients of each sandwich to get to know each other better, thereby blending their unique personalities to perfection. Open wide. Ahhhh! Don't' try to talk...no one would understand what you're saying anyway. All you need to complete this meal is some chilled fresh fruit and a big pile of napkins.

****

Boy, finding ANYTHING about the history of peppers was quite a task. I can tell you this, a <u>red</u> <u>pepper</u> is just a green pepper that was left on the plant to ripen. The reason they usually cost more than their green cousin is...it takes a lot more time, 30-45 days, for them to ripen.

As far as I could discover, they were domesticated in Mexico. The jalapenos have been traced back 6,000 years. Columbus brought peppers back to Europe where they quickly became very popular.

As I was doing my research, I discovered green and red peppers are used in recipes all over the world...from the Balkan Islands to Turkey to Japan. Almost every cultures' recipes include both sweet and hot peppers. Amazing! In Creole cooking, green peppers, celery and onions make up what is known as the "Holy Trinity."

Florida is the largest producer of peppers in the United States. They devote 19,554 acres to these globe-shaped vegetables, while Texas comes in second with almost 5,000 acres.

Red peppers are sweeter than green peppers and although they both are an important source of Antioxidants, red peppers have a more significant level of Vitamin A than their green counterparts. Not only does the level of Vitamin A increase as the peppers ripen, so does the level of Vitamin C. Sweet peppers have 530IU of Vitamin A per cup. While the same amount of hot peppers have a whopping 8,062IU!!! Now we know why hot peppers are so good for you.

When I was young I used to hate the taste of green peppers. My Mom tried making stuffed peppers when I was about 8 years old. My brothers and I put up such a fuss, she never made them again (and we weren't picky eaters). Now I love them. So all you Moms out there...take heart. It might be just a matter of time before your kids and their taste buds grow up and they become absolutely enamored with the world of vegetables. Well...they might.

JOYFUL VEGGIE CHEESE PICNIC SANDWICHES
(Serves 4-6)

These can be made ahead (1 day at the most) and refrigerated. Set them out for about 1/2 hour before you serve them. They're best not too chilly.

4-6 good sandwich rolls*
Cream Cheese Filling:
1 8 oz. pkg. neufatchel cheese, softened
2 T. fresh <u>basil</u>, cut into slivers (2 t. dry)
1 t. fresh oregano, chopped (1/2 t. dry)
1 large clove garlic, smashed

Beat all of the ingredients together until smooth. Set aside. Do not refrigerate. The flavors will start to blend as you make the Veggie Filling.

Veggie Filling:
2-3 T. infused olive oil (See next page) or regular olive oil
1 medium sweet onion, sliced
1 medium red pepper, seeded and cut into long strips
1 medium yellow pepper, seeded and cut into long strips
1 head garlic, peeled and separated into cloves...cut the really large cloves in half
Salt & pepper to taste

1.) Sauté onion and peppers in olive oil over medium heat until onion begins to turn transparent.
2.) Add the garlic and continue to cook, stirring all the time to make sure the garlic doesn't burn. You may be wondering if this isn't too much garlic for one recipe...well, you might need a mint or two after you have

one of these sandwiches BUT when garlic is cooked the way you're doing it now, a sweet, nutty flavor replaces its strong taste. Plus think of all the good you're doing your arteries. OK, continue to sauté until the onion and the peppers start to turn a nice golden brown. Add salt and pepper to taste. Remove from the heat and cool slightly...about 15 minutes should do it.

3.) Assembly time. The kids could help you with this. Liberally spread the herby cream cheese on one side of your yummy roll. Top with the veggie mixture. These are soooo good!

*This is a happy way to get your kids to eat their veggies. If you have small children, you could use small rolls for them.

****

Here comes <u>basil</u>! Did you know the Greek word for basil means "king?" It is an *herbe royale* in France, while in Italy it is a sign of love. When a woman puts a pot of basil on the balcony outside her room, she is ready to receive her lover. In India, people worship basil more highly than kings. It is considered a sacred herb dedicated to the gods Vishnu and Krishna.

You can tell by the squared stem, it is a member of the mint family and is commonly used by herbalists for an upset stomach or to get rid of gas. Steep a teaspoon of the dried leaves (use a tea ball) in a cup of boiling water. Basil tea also helps with cramps, vomiting and constipation. You can chew on a basil leaf (macerate) and put it on a painful insect sting...it works very well on spider bites too...to relieve the pain. A cup of basil tea can bring on delayed menstruation, however pregnant women should NOT drink it.

Basil is another one of the herbs I don't ever want to be without. It's easy to grow indoors in a pot in a sunny window. Every summer I grow at least 4 different kinds. This year I have a huge traditional basil, a cinnamon, a Thai and a lemon basil. In the Joyful Veggie Cheese Picnic Sandwich recipe, it calls for infused oil. I will tell you how to make it. When my step-daughter and I were in Switzerland a very nice young waiter told us how. In the restaurant we were at, every table had a bottle of infused oil the patrons were dipping endless amounts of bread into. Neither of us had ever had olive oil that way before. It was heavenly. OK, here goes.

Infused olive oil: In a sterilized 32 ounce bottle, put the following...a couple large sprigs of basil, slightly bruised to release the flavor; 1 T. peppercorns; 6 cloves of garlic, nicked with a knife and a couple of bruised sprigs of oregano. Pour olive oil over, covering the herbs completely. Cork tightly and set in a sunny window for two weeks, gently shaking it every couple of days to enhance the flavor of the oil. The oil must always cover the herbs. It will mold if it does not. Then you have to pitch it out and start over. Refrigerate the oil between uses to keep it food safe. Olive oil solidifies in the fridge so you need to let it sit at room temp or in a pan of warm water before you want to use it. It sounds like a pain but it really is worth the effort...and the flavor. As an added bonus you save lots of money when you make it yourself. Infused oils in gourmet stores can be expensive. Always use sterilized bottles. OK?

STEAMY NIGHT SANDWICHES
(Makes 4 big sandwiches)

The humidity can be unreal here in the Midwest. The last thing you want to do is get near a stove...on or off. This sandwich was created for those hot, steamy nights when you don't have enough energy to put together much of anything.

4 Kaiser rolls

Herbed Cheese Spread:
8 oz. neufatchel cheese, softened
1 t. dehydrated onion
1 T. fresh marjoram, 1 t. dry
A couple shakes of Louisiana Hot Sauce
1 clove garlic, crushed

1.) Whip all this together until well blended. Set aside.

The rest of the ingredients:
Your favorite honey mustard
1 small sweet onion, thinly sliced
1 large tomato, sliced
1/2 C. jicama, thinly sliced
Some red leaf lettuce

1.) Split each roll in half. Spread honey mustard on the top half and *Herbed Cheese Spread* on the bottom half.
2.) Layer the onion, tomato, jicama, and lettuce on top of the cheese spread. Put the top on. You're all set. This has become one of my

favorite sandwiches because it's fast and tastes so cool and crunchy after a long hot day.

Now pour some iced tea, go outside on your patio or deck and have a relaxing meal with your family or friends. This sandwich is perfect with my no-cooking-needed, *Could Be Spicy Bean Salad.*

****

It was a little tricky to find much historical information on jicama . The word, itself, is derived from the Aztec word, Xicamatl. Jicama is native to Mexico and northern Central America. It is one of Mexico's and southeast Asia's major crops and is called the Mexican potato. Here is a little known tidbit. You know that thickener, "arrowroot?" It's jicama! Fancy that. If memory serves me aren't there teething biscuits for babies made of arrowroot?

Anyway...some people who eat a lot of it, have trouble digesting it. You have to eat an awful lot to get to that point though. Jicama is quickly becoming one of the vegetables used on a vegetable and dip tray. I love it's mildly, sweet crunchiness. It's high in Fiber, has lots of Vitamin C, is low in Sodium and has only 45 Calories in 2 cups! Unless of course you like to dip it in French onion or ranch dip first.

I can't remember when I first had jicama...it sort of crept into my cooking very unobtrusively. It's great in salads, on sandwiches, in stir fry, or just plain. I think it tastes sort of like raw peas but most other people think it tastes like an apple. Whatever you think, go ahead and try it. Just remember to peel it first.

GRILLED ZUCCHINI CHEESE SANDWICHES
(Serves 2)

This is for two sandwiches, but it can easily be adapted to any amount you need. I've used rye, pumpernickel, 7-grain and sourdough bread with this recipe. Whatever makes your tummy sing will be perfect.

2 T. olive oil
1 medium zucchini, thinly sliced lengthwise
4 large whole garlic cloves, peeled and sliced
Salt and pepper to taste
A little _butter_
6 large fresh basil leaves, you could use a sprinkle of dry
2 oz. chihuahua, brick or muenster cheese, sliced
4 slices of good bread

1.) Heat skillet for 30-40 seconds, then add oil.
2.) Sauté zucchini over medium high heat. When zucchini starts to get soft, add garlic. Lower heat. Turn zucchini slices and stir garlic frequently to keep it from burning. Cook until they both are a gentle golden brown. Drain on paper towels.
3.) Sprinkle zucchini with a little salt and pepper.
4.) Lightly _butter_ 2 slices of bread. Place buttered side down on skillet. Don't turn on the heat yet.
5.) Arrange zucchini and cooked garlic on each of the slices of bread. Top with basil and finally the cheese.
6.) Butter the other two slices of bread and place buttered side up on top of the cheese.
7.) Grill the sandwiches over a low flame. Keep a close watch so it doesn't burn. If the bread starts to get too dark before the cheese

has started to melt, lower the flame. Flip it when the color is a beeyoootiful golden brown. Grill the other side. The trick to perfectly grilled sandwiches is to not let the heat get too high so the cheese has a chance to melt AND frequent checking to get it exactly the way you want.

This is a perfect sandwich for a cool, crisp autumn day...especially with a bowl of your favorite homemade soup. Don't forget to wear your slippers. Comfy? I'll bet you are.

****

Butter is mentioned in the Bible. It was probably used by all people who had reached the pastoral stage of development. Nomads have prepared it from many different kinds of milk, including buffaloes and camels. Among earliest Greeks and Romans, butter was scarce due to lack of pasture land and not the right type of cow. During the Middle Ages, the Scandinavians are believed to be the first to use butter extensively as food. They introduced it to the rest of Europe and that was that. The use of butter spread quickly.

It takes nine quarts of milk to make 1 pound of butter. Have you ever tried to make butter yourself? My Mom used to be a kindergarten teacher. She had her class make butter by passing an old peanut butter jar, filled with whipping cream around her class. It was up to each individual student to shake the jar as long as they could and then pass it on to the next child. Around and around the class that jar went until...butter. She strained off most of the liquid and the solid that remained was butter. A couple of her students were very concerned because it didn't look like what they had at home. Mom mixed in a few drops of yellow food coloring and they were soothed. They each had some spread on a cracker and were actually quite proud of themselves. They'd made butter!

137

Butter is at least 80% Fat, the rest is water. The yellow color usually comes from carotene, annatto, or marigolds. I love the flavor of butter. You can definitely tell when something else has been used in place of it. One of the tricks I've learned over years of cooking, is if you add the butter at the very end of the cooking process, to... say, your just cooked vegetables, all you need is a little bit to get the flavor many of us love. When I was in France, the French love it so much, they spread butter on their meat...and they're all skinny!

I'd rather have the real thing, than some of that other stuff that's out there. I get pretty suspicious when the ingredients sound like something from a high school chemistry class. I like my food to be as close to it's natural state as possible.

AS FOR BUTTER VS MARGARINE, I TRUST COWS MORE THAN CHEMISTS.
-Joan Gussow

GLORIOUSLY CRUNCHY WRAPS
(Serves 3-4)

Soaked sunflower seeds add such a special flavor and literally make this wrap come ALIVE!!!!

*Soak 1/4 C. raw sunflowers seeds, in 1 C. of pure water for at least 6 hours. Do this first thing in the morning, and they'll be ready when it's time to start dinner. Drain before using.

1 C. carrot, peeled & grated

2 stalks celery, grated

3 green onions, thinly sliced

1/3 C. black olives, sliced

4 large tortillas or 6 large romaine lettuce leaves

6 radishes, grated

1 medium green pepper, seeded and grated

1 medium tomato, sliced

*Soaked sunflower seeds

Cheese spread:

6 oz. neufatchel cheese, softened

1 T. fresh dill, snipped into very tiny pieces

1 large clove garlic, crushed

1 t. honey

Milk to thin

1.) Grate the carrot, radishes, celery, and green pepper into a medium sized bowl. A salad shooter or food processor will make short work of this.

2.) Add the green onions and black olives. Mix well.

3.) Beat all the *Cheese spread* ingredients, except the milk, together with a hand mixer. Thin with milk, usually 2 T., to get a nice spreading consistency.

4.) Now take a tortilla or lettuce leaf, spread it with some of the cheese spread, next pile on some of the grated veggies, top with tomato slices and soaked sunflower seeds.

5.) Finally, roll it up. I, myself, prefer the lettuce leaves...mess or no mess. I make sure I have lots of napkins. Aren't those soaked sunflower seeds the freshest things you've ever eaten? You can add them to salads, sprinkle them on your oatmeal, put them in smoothies, whatever you like.

****

The radish is one of the oldest known cultivated plants, is part of the mustard family and has very little nutritional value. It was held in such high esteem by the ancient Greeks, that small replicas of the radish were made in gold, in connection with worship of Apollo. Maria Callas, one of the greatest dramatic sopranos of all time, and of Greek origin, had an interesting experience after one of her performances. Members of the audience threw radishes on the stage. She graciously picked them up and held them to her as she took her bow. Obviously those radishes were a symbol of great love and respect.

For thousands of years the radish was used as an appetite stimulant. The Roman poet, Horace, said it was "a vegetable to excite the languid stomach." Ben Johnson, a contemporary of Shakespeare, thought it was good to eat them before drinking wine. I, myself, have never tried that.

The earliest reference comes from China during the 7th Century B.C. where radishes grew in the cooler regions. They then spread into the Mediterranean region, then on to Europe and were brought to the Americas in the late 1500's or early 1600's.

All types of radishes are common to the cuisines of Russia, China, India, the Middle East, Mexico, Europe and North America. There is an annual radish festival in Mexico I thought sounded interesting. It's called Noches de los Rabano, Night of the Radishes. It is held each year in Oaxaca, Mexico on December 23, and has been a focal point of Christmas celebrations for over a century. Check out the radish sculptures and other information on the website: www.planeta.com/ecotravel/mexico/oaxaca/rabanos. All you radish lovers, start planning your next vacation.

My first experience with radishes was when I was a little girl. My Dad loved cottage cheese and radish sandwiches. Now don't get excited. He'd toast a nice slice of rye bread, put cottage cheese on it and slice radishes on top of that. Next a little sprinkle of salt and pepper and that was it. Normally most kids would wrinkle up their noses at such a creation but my Dad was smart. He told my brothers and I it was only a sandwich for adults. We would have to acquire a taste for it because our immature taste buds weren't ready for such a grown up experience. Well of course you know what that meant. We had to try one immediately, otherwise we could not go on living. Don't knock it...they're fabulous.

EDIBLE FLOWER TEA SANDWICHES
(Makes 20-25 open-faced sandwiches)

I love to have tea parties with my friends. Since I am an organic gardener, I always have a variety of herbs and edible flowers to pick from for these sandwiches. At first some of my friends didn't want to eat flowers but since they are all fairly adventurous, they decided to give it a whirl. I could tell by their faces they were pleasantly surprised.

1 8oz. cream cheese, softened
1 clove garlic, crushed
1 T. fresh herbs, chopped very fine*
20-25 slices cocktail bread, you choose the flavor
1 C. edible flowers**

1.) Combine cream cheese, garlic and herbs (ex. basil and oregano or cilantro and chives or dill and parsley). Beat with electric mixer for 2 minutes.

2.) Spread mixture on bread and decorate with herbs and flowers. Use each slice of bread as an individual canvas. Get creative and have fun. If you're not serving them immediately, they'll need to be refrigerated. The flowers tend to wilt after an hour or so if they're not cold.

*Examples of herbs that are compatible with edible flowers: Dill, Parsley, Chives, Burnett, Cilantro, Basil, Oregano and flowering tips from Lemon Verbena or Tarragon.

**Examples of edible flowers: Pansies, Roses, Violas, Violets, Snapdragons, Nasturtiums, Borage flowers, any flowers from scented geraniums and Chive flowers.

142

Note: Most of the flowers have a mild cucumber-like taste, except the Nasturtium which is spicy and the Snapdragon which is sweet. Also, make sure to use flowers and herbs that have not been sprayed with pesticides or other chemicals.

****

Dill's history goes way back. Ancient Egyptian medical texts, dating back to 3,000 BC, mention it. The old Norse derivative of dill, dilla, meant to soothe or calm. It was used in many old cultures to get rid of gas, to calm the stomach and to increase a nursing mother's milk.

Long ago, it was considered by the Romans, to be a sign of luck and by the Greeks to be a symbol of wealth. Medieval folklore believed that dried dill seeds, hung in doorways in the home or above a baby's cradle, symbolized love and provided protection. Mystics thought they could combat the "evil eye" by carrying a bag of dried dill over their hearts.

Today European and American herbalists use both the leaves and seeds in many of the same ways the ancient herbalists did. They also use dill to stimulate a sluggish appetite and relieve babies suffering from colic.

Two hundred or so years ago, when church services were hours long, parents used to have their kids chew on dill seeds to keep them calm and alert during sermons. Because of this, dill seeds were often referred to as "meetin' seeds."

I have grown dill for years and will give you a heads up if you want to grow it in your garden. I did not know how prolific dill can be. Mature dill plants have huge seed heads. If you do not cut those heads off, they will self-sow the following spring and you will have dill everywhere!!! Do I sound like the voice of

143

experience? Even baby dill plants have long tap roots which are very hard to pull up if they are growing where you don't want them to.

Don't let this dissuade you from trying dill. It is a beautiful plant with feathery leaves that are exquisite in salads, deviled eggs, or in a yogurt sauce to accompany grilled fish. Use kitchen scissors to snip the leaves instead of chopping with a knife. I think scissors work better. When I make rye bread I substitute dill seeds for caraway seeds. One tablespoon of dill seeds steeped in a cup of boiling water is wonderful for an upset stomach. A tablespoon of dill seeds has the same amount of Calcium as 1/3 C. milk.

One summer I was privileged to have a whole bunch of monarch caterpillars use some of my dill as host plants to munch and spin cocoons on. I don't think dill is their usual host plant because that never happened again.

Chapter 6

Salads and Salad Dressings

Family reunion, 1959

MARY ANNE'S SHRIMP SALAD
(Serves 4)

This is shrimply delicious and so easy to make. I love this on a hot summer night with a fresh loaf of crusty French bread and blueberry iced tea. Mary Anne, whom I've known forever, loves seafood. When she created this salad, shrimp, by far and away, is the star ingredient.

1 lb. cooked <u>shrimp</u>
2 stalks celery, finely diced
1/2 red pepper, finely diced
1/2 cucumber, finely diced
2 small green onions, sliced

1 hard boiled egg, chopped
2 C. cooked tiny shell pasta
1/2 C. mayonnaise
1-3 t. curry powder to taste
Salt and pepper to taste

1.) Put the <u>shrimp</u>, celery, red pepper, cucumber, green onions, hard boiled egg, and pasta in a good sized salad bowl. Mix it together gently.
2.) Whisk the curry into the mayonnaise. Add some salt and pepper if you like.
3.) Pour the dressing over the rest of the shrimp salad. Mix well. Chill for about one hour so the flavors have a chance to blend. You are going to luuuv this!

HAPPINESS IS LIKE A KISS-
IN ORDER TO GET ANY GOOD OUT OF IT
YOU HAVE TO GIVE IT TO SOMEONE ELSE.

The ancient Greeks and Romans loved <u>shrimp</u> and preferred the large ones to lobster. One of their favorite ways to cook them was to wrap them in fig leaves and steam them. I never tried that before. Anybody got a fig leaf? In Copenhagen, shrimp and a slice of buttered bread are sold from pushcarts. In Japan they can be bought from street stands, swiftly decapitated and eaten raw. The English consider a prawn to be a shrimp that is over 3 inches long. That's a very big shrimp!

New Orleans is the premier shrimp-eating city in the U.S. This luscious little critter is the most popular crustacean by far in the States. We eat over 500 million pounds annually!!!

I think the best shrimp cocktail I ever had was in San Francisco, by the bay, from a vendor who had set up a cart near the wax museum. The shrimp, caught that morning, were so succulent and big. Anybody know if they still do that? Is the wax museum still there? There's nothing like having a fabulous shrimp cocktail while the beauty of San Francisco surrounds you and the fresh, salty scent of San Francisco Bay is mesmerizing your olfactory nerves. You have got to try it.

A 3 ounce portion of shrimp is 90 Calories, only 10 of those Calories are from Fat. They are high in Iron and Protein but low in Carbohydrates. There are 247 mg. of Potassium in each 3 ounce serving. Shrimp are so versatile, I'll bet you have a favorite way to eat them too.

GOOD HEALTH IS THE THING THAT
MAKES YOU FEEL THAT NOW
IS THE VERY BEST TIME OF YEAR.

SUNSHINE SALAD WITH ORANGE VINAIGRETTE
(Serves 4-6)

This salad radiates and dances in your mouth whether it's sunny or cloudy outside. Remember to soak your sunflower seeds first thing in the morning. Once you've tasted soaked sunflower seeds, you'll want to use them all the time in other recipes.

Salad:
2 large heads Boston lettuce
2 <u>oranges</u>, peeled and cut in chunks or segments
1/2 C. soaked sunflower seeds*
1 C. slivered almonds, toasted**

2 green onions, chopped
1 can sliced water chestnuts, drained
1 avocado, cubed

Orange Vinaigrette:
1/2 C. grape seed or safflower oil
1/4 C. rice wine vinegar
2 T. fresh orange juice
1 clove garlic, crushed
1/2 t. salt
1/8 t. pepper
1 t. honey
A bit of orange peel...not too much

*Note: Put the ½ C. sunflower seeds in a jar with a lid. Add water to cover. Put the lid on and soak for at least 6 hours. Drain off water before using in salad.

**Note: To toast almonds, put them in a large non-stick frying pan and turn the heat to medium. Stirring constantly, toast the almonds until you can start to smell their warm nuttiness. This should take around 5-7 minutes. Taste...careful...they're hot. If they're not done yet, turn the heat down a bit. You've got to be careful when you're toasting nuts, you don't want them to burn.

1.) Toss all the salad ingredients, except the almonds, in a large bowl.
2.) Put all the vinaigrette ingredients in a 16 oz. jar with a lid. Put the lid on. Shake. Pretty simple, huh?
3.) Put the dressing on about 10 minutes before you're going to serve. Top with almonds. Everybody, Tango!!!

****

The first <u>oranges</u> were bitter and growing wild in China, where references appear as early as 2,500 B.C. It is thought the Chinese began cultivating them about this time. Why the orange remained in the Orient for thousands of years is unclear. Early records make no mention of it in the Middle East or in ancient Greece. After the fall of Rome, the Romans brought young trees back to Rome, by long sea voyages. Raising and exporting oranges was in it's infancy when it faded from history for centuries. Again...no record of what happened.

The Moors, the Muslim natives of North Africa, brought oranges with them to southern Spain in the 8th and 9th Centuries. Finally they caught on. By the 1200's orange groves were plentiful between Seville and Granada, as well as parts of Portugal. The Saracens, another Muslim group, introduced orange growing in Sicily. It was Columbus who brought them to the Americas in 1493.

The Bigarade, the bitter kind, is believed to be the parent of all oranges.

When the sweet orange was introduced in Europe over 500 years ago, the bitter one was immediately booted out. Because of its hardiness, the bitter orange served for centuries, as root stock for the sweet variety. Have you ever been to Arizona where orange trees are everywhere? The smell of orange blossoms is so intoxicating it will take your breath away. I made the mistake of tasting an orange from what is now considered an "ornamental tree." EWWW! I can see why they were given the boot.

90% of Florida oranges are made into juice. California produces the most eating oranges in the United States. Today, Brazil supplies 50% of the world's orange juice, with the Netherlands being its #1 customer. Brazil's orange growing industry almost went belly up during World War II, but they were able to turn it around...big time. Way to go Brazil!

As far as nutrition...well, a medium-sized orange has only 62 Calories, 269 mg of Vitamin A, 69.7 mg Vitamin C, 39.7 mcg Folic Acid, 52 mg Calcium and 237 mg Potassium. Nutritious little bugger isn't it? It's a great way to get some nutrition into your kids and grandkids...not to mention yourself.

BLISSFUL FRUIT SALAD
(Serves 3-4)

All fruit salad is not created equal. Somehow I stumbled onto this combination of fruits and my tongue was amazed. There is something very special about this union that will make your tonsils sing...even if you don't have any.

1 C. sliced strawberries

2 nectarines, sliced then cut in chunks

1 1/2 C. blueberries

1 banana, sliced

*Edible flowers, optional

1 C. mango, cut in chunks

2 peeled and sliced kiwi

1 C. green seedless grapes

2 Friar plums (the deep, red ones) sliced, then cut in chunks

Use fruits that are perfectly ripe so you can experience the full flavor of this gorgeous salad.

1.) Mix all the fruits together except the banana and the edible flowers. Don't prepare this salad too far ahead. If you want your salad chilled, refrigerate the whole, unprepared fruit (except the banana) for at least 4 hours before you need them.

2.) Just before serving, slice the banana into the rest of the fruit and mix gently.

3.) For some fun and an unexpected twist, add some edible flowers. Make sure they haven't been sprayed. Don't use flowers you get at the grocery store unless they're labeled edible. Use them from your own garden where you will know if they've been sprayed or not.

*Some examples of edible flowers are violets, borage flowers, pansies, rose

petals, johnny-jump-ups, snap dragons and mint flowers. Nasturtiums are also very edible but would not go well with the fruit. They have a very peppery taste...unless that, of course, appeals to you.

I usually pick the flowers first thing in the morning, wash them carefully and throw out any that are a little brown around the edges. Check for bugs, then put them in a plastic bag and place them in your fridge until you're ready to use them.

****

Nectarines are one of the oldest fruits. They originated over 2,000 years ago in China and were cultivated in ancient Persia, Greece and Rome. They were brought to Europe from Persia and were introduced in Great Britain near the end of the 16th Century. Nectarines were brought to America by the Spanish and were grown in Australia from the early days of European settlement.

They are a fuzzless variety of peach, a member of the rose family (!) and also related to almonds. They are, however, not a cross between a peach and a plum. A funny thing about peaches and nectarines is...sometimes nectarines will appear on peach trees and sometimes peaches will show up on nectarine trees. They're not into boundaries, I guess.

I found a great quote from the famous English poet, John Keats. He said the following while eating a nectarine: "Talking of pleasure, this moment I was writing with one hand and with the other holding to my mouth a nectarine-good God, how fine! It went down soft , pulpy, slushy, oozy-all its delicious embodiment melted down my throat like a large beautiful strawberry. I shall certainly breed." I couldn't have said it better myself, although I'm not sure about the breeding part. The word nectarine means 'sweet as nectar'-food of the gods. There are more than 100 varieties. Have you ever had perfectly ripe white nectarines? They don't have as much beta carotene as the yellow variety, but the flavor is out of this world. We happened on some fabulous ones at the grocery store, which is really pretty rare for the Midwest. Most of the fruit looks great but it's usually dry, flavorless and mealy. Anyway, these white nectarines had a flavor like none I've ever experienced. They were almost perfum-y and sweet and juicy. We savored every bite.

California produces 95% of the ones grown in the United States. One nectarine has 1001 iu of Vitamin A. It also has lots of Vitamin C, Beta Carotene and Potassium. I know, I know, you're just dying to have one now...aren't you?

SERENDIPITOUS SHRIMP SALAD
(Makes 4 large servings)

This is wonderful served with my New Dawn Salad Dressing (p. 183). All you need is some great bread and fresh fruit. This salad has a few what I call "adventurous" ingredients that are very appealing when they're mixed together. I'll bet this will become one of your favorite salads.

1 large head of red leaf lettuce, washed, dried and torn into bite-sized pieces
1 can hearts of palm, drained and cut into 1" pieces
1 15 oz. can garbanzo beans, drained and rinsed
1 C. carrots, peeled and sliced into rounds
1 C. celery, thinly sliced
1 C. jicama, peeled and cut julienne style
3 green onions, sliced, including part of the green
1 lb. fresh shrimp, cooked, shelled and de-veined
2 hard boiled eggs, sliced
3 oz. low-fat jack cheese, cubed
1 avocado, cubed

1.) Prepare all the ingredients and toss them together UNLESS you are making this ahead or want to serve it chilled. If that's the case, add the avocado just before serving.

2.) If you're in a hurry and don't have time to make a salad dressing, your favorite ranch or French dressing will do just fine.

DID YOU EVER STOP TO TASTE A CARROT? NOT JUST EAT IT, BUT TASTE IT? YOU CAN'T TASTE THE BEAUTY AND THE ENERGY OF THE EARTH IN A TWINKIE.

-Astrid Alauda

If you've never tried <u>hearts of palm</u>, you're really missing something. You can find them in your grocery store by the canned artichoke hearts, which are usually by the olives. Hearts of palm are actually the heart of the sabal Palmetto, a tall, tough-barked palm that just so happens to be the Florida State Tree. It used to be called "swamp cabbage" by Floridians and was regarded as poor man's food. During the Depression these trees were aggressively cut down as a source of food, which was pretty incredible since the bark is extremely tough and the chain saw had not yet been invented.

It wasn't long, however, before hearts of palm's extreme tenderness and delicacy was noticed. It went from being "swamp cabbage" to "millionaire's salad" almost over night. In fact, Florida had to enact a state law to protect the tree from hungry gourmets.

Hearts of palm have thrived for thousands of years throughout Central and South America. At the time Columbus arrived in the New World, the Carib Indians were taking full advantage of what they called the Pejibaye tree. They made houses from its bark, put a roof over their heads with the leaves, ate the nuts from the mature trees and ate the center core of the young plants.

Today this tree is grown as a cash crop in Central and South America, especially Brazil. The tree needs 150 inches of rain per year to thrive and cannot handle freezing weather. At 12 months, when it is 5 feet tall and 4 inches in diameter, it is harvested.

One cup of hearts of palm contains 41 Calories, 1g. Fat, 0 Trans Fats, 0 Cholesterol, 4g. Fiber, 58mg. Calcium, and 3g. Protein. It also contains 622mg. Sodium. If you are watching your salt intake, go easy.

One of my favorite ways to eat it is simply to cut it up in pieces, pour a great French dressing over it and a couple grinds of fresh black pepper. Ahhh! Lunch is served quickly, and what a treat.

AYE KARUMBA PASTA SALAD
(Serves 6-8)

Make this at least two hours ahead so the flavors have time to blend. While the salad is chilling, get out your Mexican hat, throw it on the floor and start dancing around it. This makes a huge salad so invite some people over and you can all dance around the hat. Ole!

1 1lb. pkg. small shell or rigatoni pasta, cooked
1 16 oz. can black beans, drained and rinsed
2 C. frozen corn, thawed, or fresh off the cob if you've got it
1 C. celery sliced
1 C. chopped red pepper
3 green onions, with part of the green, chopped
2-3 T. fresh cilantro or parsley
Salt & pepper to taste

Dressing:
1 C. lo-fat or full fat mayo, your choice
1 C. non-fat sour cream
1 1/2 t. chili powder
2 t. cumin
2 cloves garlic, crushed
1 1/2 C. chunky salsa, homemade or store bought
Milk, if needed

1.) First thing is to get that pasta cooked so it's ready when you need it. After it's done, run it under cold water or give it an ice bath to cool it down quickly.

2.) Put the black beans, corn, celery, red pepper, green onions and cilantro into a large bowl. Toss gently. Add the drained pasta when it's cooled. This is the time to add salt to taste and lots of freshly ground pepper.

3.) You can make the dressing as fat or as skinny as you like. Whisk the mayonnaise and sour cream together. Stir in the rest of the dressing ingredients. If it is too thick, thin it with a little milk.

4.) Pour the dressing over the salad. Mix well. Taste. As the flavors blend, this salad gets better and better. Chilled, sliced mangoes are the perfect accompaniment.

****

We are going to address <u>beans</u> in general here...but not the green bean. You know, like kidney beans, navy beans, garbanzo beans, etc. The late Senator Everett Dirksen was highly affronted when he ordered bean soup in the Senate Dining Room only to discover there was none on the menu. "The senator promptly introduced a resolution to the effect that henceforth, not a day should pass when the Senate was in session and the restaurant open, that there would not be bean soup on the menu. It has therefore become an inviolate practice and glorious tradition that the humble little bean should always be honored." _The All American Bean Book_, by F.H. "Ted" Waskey.

Beans have been traced back to the Bronze Age in Switzerland. They were a favorite food among the early Greeks and their Trojan rivals. So popular were beans in ancient Egypt that temples were dedicated to them, where the bean was worshipped as a symbol of life itself. Among the early Jews, beans were eaten 1,000 years before the dawn of the Christian era. The Romans even gambled with them.

Archaeologists think beans are native to Peru. Dried beans have been found in pre-Columbian tombs and Egyptian pyramids. From Peru it is thought they were introduced throughout the world by soldiers who carried them as a staple of their diet while they fought ancient wars...just like American GI's did during World War II. Strong evidence suggests American Indians were growing fields of beans, as well as maize and squash, long before Columbus got to America.

My best childhood bean memory comes from a friend of my Mom's. Gail was the baked bean queen of my hometown. She started with dried beans and went from there, adding onion, molasses, brown sugar and other magical ingredients. She would bake them slowly for hours, until they were rich and gooey. Her house smelled like heaven and they were fabulous. No matter how big a pot she used, they were always gone...to the last bean.

Nutritionally, beans are the richest and most inexpensive source of vegetable protein when cooked. 1/2 C. of cooked beans has only 118 Calories and is loaded with B Vitamins, Fiber, Iron, Calcium, Phosphorus and Potassium. So, now you can consider the bean, not a lowly bean, but SUPER BEAN.

LENTIL PASTA SALAD
(Serves an army of 8-10)

This recipe makes a ton, but it won't last long. If any is left over, it's even better the next day.

1 C. lentils, rinsed and picked over
1 lb. angel hair pasta, cooked
2 C. frozen baby peas, thawed
4 green onions, including green part, sliced
3 C. romaine lettuce, roughly chopped
1 sweet red pepper, sliced julienne
1/2 C. cilantro, chopped (use parsley if you don't like cilantro)
1 C. toasted almonds

Dressing:

1 T. honey
5-6 shakes Louisiana hot sauce
4 T. rice wine vinegar
1 t. ground ginger
1/2 C. safflower oil

1 t. Dijon mustard
1 T. water
4 cloves garlic, crushed
4 T. liquid aminos
2 T. sesame oil

1.) Cook the pasta and rinse under cold water as soon as it's done. Put in large bowl.

2.) While you're waiting for the pasta water to boil, rinse the lentils and pick out any funny looking ones, also check over for small stones. Put the lentils in a pan with 2 1/2 C. water and 1/2 t. salt. Cook over low heat for 20-25 minutes. Drain and rinse under cold water. Put in the bowl with the pasta.

3.) While you're waiting for the lentils and pasta to cook, why not prepare the vegetables. Add the peas, green onions, lettuce, red pepper, and cilantro or parsley to the bowl.

4.) Put all the dressing ingredients into an empty 16 oz. jar with a lid. Make sure the lid is screwed on tight. OK, shake your bootie. Do a dance around the kitchen.

5.) Pour the dressing over it all. Toss gently, making sure everything is well mixed. Chill for at least an hour or so. All the ingredients get to know each other and become really good friends. Toss the almonds in just before serving. Invite someone over you haven't seen in a while. They'll love this.

****

Lentils are the Rodney Dangerfield of dried beans...they don't get much respect. Throughout history, some cultures considered them the food of the poor people. As early as 5,000 years ago, Egyptians were loving their lentils. They were lentil traders and probably introduced them to the Greeks and Romans. 2.8 million pounds of lentils were once used, as packing, to send a carved stone obelisk from Egypt to Rome. The obelisk still stands in front of St. Peter's Basilica in Vatican City.

In ancient Greece, where lentils were considered the food of the poor, the wealthy would never have thought to serve them at their dinner tables, except for Hippocrates, the father of medicine, who prescribed them for liver ailments.

Lentils are not very popular in the United States, but they are very important to the diets of the Middle East and India. For centuries the French have honored the lentil for use in soup. It is thought the French were the ones to introduce lentils to northern America. The Iroquois of the St. Lawrence Valley grew them in abundance from the 1700's on.

I think lentil soup is one of the most inviting soups on a cold winter day. I love the smell of my kitchen when a pot of vegetable lentil soup is simmering on the stove and the north wind is blustering around outside. I'll invite a couple friends over and we'll sit happily at my kitchen table sopping up lentil soup with homemade cheese cornbread...now doesn't that sound comfy?

Lentils are second to the soybean in Protein content. They are rich in B Vitamins, Phosphorus and Iron. They also have 358 mcg. of Folic Acid, 730 mg. Potassium, and 5.5 mcg. Selenium per cup! Nutritious little buggers. Another thing that isn't well known about lentils is they're wonderful sprouted. I usually sprout 1/4 C. lentils in 1 C. water, in a jar, overnight. I drain the water out in the morning, add fresh water and give them a shake or two during the day if I'm home. Some times I replace the water one more time. By the time dinner rolls around, they're ready to toss into a salad. Just drain them and they're all set. You have to try this because the taste is hard to describe. It's such a fresh taste, your mouth just pops and giggles. Go on, try it.

COULD BE SPICY, BEAN SALAD
(Serves 6-8)

This is a fast, no-cooking-needed salad that is just bursting with all kind of electrifying flavors. How spicy it is depends, on how hot the salsa you're using is and how much cayenne pepper you add to the dressing.

1 15-20 oz. can each; kidney beans, garbanzo beans, and black beans
3 C. corn, you could use canned or fresh off the cob or frozen and thawed
3 stalks of celery, sliced
1 4 oz. can, mild green chili peppers, chopped
1 C. of your favorite salsa
1 C. black olives, sliced
1/2 C. fresh cilantro, chopped
3 green onions sliced using part of the green

1.) Throw all the ingredients into a large bowl. Blend, baby, blend.
2.) Make the Dressing.
3.) Chill for at least one hour. The longer this one marinates, the better it is. It's still terrific 3 days later...if there's any left.

Dressing:
2/3 C. safflower oil
1/3 C. tarragon vinegar (see "how to" in Teas and Other Diddies Section at the back of the book) or red wine vinegar
3 cloves garlic, pressed
1 T. fresh lime juice

1 1/2 t. cumin
1-2 t. chili powder
1/8-1/2 t. cayenne pepper, or more if you like
1/2 t. dry tarragon
3-4 grinds fresh pepper
1-2 t. salt

4.) Put all the Dressing ingredients in a 16 oz. jar with a lid. Shake until mixed thoroughly and pour over salad. Stir, making sure the dressing and salad ingredients are combined from top to bottom. Use those muscles. Serve with your favorite tortilla chips...you won't even need a fork or a spoon.

****

Celery was first used as a medicine to treat nervousness and is thought to be the plant, selinon, that Homer mentioned in the Odyssey in 850 B.C. Hippocrates, who lived from around 460 B.C. to 377 B.C., prescribed it to increase urine flow. As you will find out further down the page, he was WAY ahead of his time. Celery is believed to have originated in the Mediterranean area. The Chinese also mention it in their writings around the 5th Century A.D.

By 1623, the French were using celery as a food flavoring. Small stalks and leaves were sometimes eaten with an oil dressing, in both Italy and France. After a while, French, Italian and English gardeners realized they could eliminate the too-strong flavor by growing the plants later in the summer or fall then keeping them into the winter. By the mid 1700's, wealthy Swedish families were enjoying the wintertime luxury of celery that had been stored in root cellars.

America's celery industry began in Kalamazoo, Michigan. The seed was brought over in the 1850's, from Scotland, and soon became a commercial crop. By the 1890's, vendors were boarding stopped trains at the Michigan Central Railroad Station and offering stalks of celery to puzzled travelers. People who remembered nothing about Kalamazoo, remembered celery. What a brilliant marketing plan!

Celery is a nutritious and medicinal dynamo.   It is loaded with Potassium, Calcium and Iron, very high in Fiber and is alkaline, which is a good thing if you tend to be a little on the acidic side. Due to the high amount of Potassium, and its diuretic effect (you go Hippocrates), celery can aid in the prevention and reduction of high blood pressure. Eaten regularly, it helps the kidneys to release toxins and waste, PLUS, celery contains the volatile oil, apiol, which is useful as a urinary antiseptic. WOW!

Do any of you remember The Frugal Gourmet? I remember him saying, on one of his shows, to pick celery that was a lighter green. It has a milder, sweeter taste and not as much Sodium. He was right. Lighter is better.   Have you ever tried sliced celery, steamed, then topped with a little olive oil, salt, pepper and a sprinkle of Parmesan cheese? You'll love it.

    Poem by Ogden Nash:
    Celery raw, develops the jaw,
    But celery stewed, is more quietly chewed.

QUICK AS A WINK SALAD
(Serves 4)

You can easily use your favorite salad dressing with this one. The simple, but unusual, combination of flavors adapts to almost anything. If you decide to use sunflower sprouts, you'll need to start them about 10-14 days before you need them. Now don't freak out here. Once you've tried them, you'll have some growing all the time. It's just a matter of getting started.

6 C. mixed greens
3 green onions, chopped
1 C. canned garbanzo beans
*1/2 C. sunflower sprouts, or your favorite sprout

2 plum tomatoes, chopped
4 oz. fresh mozzarella, cut into cubes
Dressing of choice

Toss all this together or if you have an attractive, glass bowl, you can layer the ingredients. It's up to you. You can make this a real work of art and it would only take a few more minutes.

Fresh mozzarella is much softer and whiter than the "normal" kind we're used to seeing in the cheese section of most of our grocery stores. Usually the fresh is shaped in a ball or a log. Many of the large grocery stores have it in the deli section. Of course if you can't find the fresh, you can always use the other kind.

I had a friend from Boston who first told me about fresh mozzarella she got from barrels on the East Coast. She said you could buy it right out of the barrel and eat it like an apple. It was more than 20 years later that I found it in the Chicago area at a Whole Foods near us.

*Chances are, you won't find sunflower sprouts at your local grocery store, but it's easy to grow them at home, inside or outside. They are more developed than the sprouts that you usually find in the grocery store, plus it takes about 10-14 days before they're just right.

OK, ready? Plant a layer of raw sunflower seeds in a large pot, using any good potting medium. Cover the seeds with about 1/2 inch of your potting medium, water and put in a sunny spot, but not direct sun. Keep them moist but not soggy. In a week or 10 days, you'll have baby plants. Cut them when they've developed into a two-leafed sprout. They'll be about 3 inches tall. If you let them go too long they get fuzzy and aren't nearly as tasty. We like to keep two pots going, one planted two weeks after the other, so we have a continuous supply. They are great on sandwiches too. I buy raw sunflower seeds at my local health food store. They are the same seeds I use to make the 6-hour sprouts in my Sunshine Salad. I'm telling you, once you taste the magic of freshly sprouted seeds, you'll have a pot and a jar going all the time. Sigh. Ain't life grand?

****

The sunflower is the only crop harvested for seed that was domesticated in the United States. Archeological evidence shows Native American Indians were cultivating sunflowers as far back as 3,000 B.C. in the Four Corners area. The seeds were pounded or ground into flour, cracked and eaten as snacks, mixed with vegetables or even squeezed for oil which was used for making bread. Medicinally, the Pawnee ground the seeds and mixed them with other herbs to strengthen the milk of pregnant women.

In 1716, an English patent had been granted for extracting oil from sunflower seeds but at this time, the sunflower was not looked at as a food plant until it reached Russia. In the early 19th Century, Russian farmers planted over 2 million acres of sunflowers. Many types of research programs were set up by the government. Credit is given to Russian immigrants for re-introducing sunflower seeds into the U.S. by the late 1800's.

Sunflower seeds and the sunflower greens (sprouts) have a slightly different nutritional value. While the seeds have more Protein, the greens have cancer-fighting Chlorophyll. They both have the B Vitamins, Vitamin E, Iron, Potassium, Phosphorus, and Magnesium. During sprouting (of many of the sprouting seeds and beans), the Vitamin and Mineral content increases a whopping 13-600%.

Go to your favorite book store and get yourself a good sprouting book. Sprouting is a good way to have ultra fresh taste and excellent nutrition easily and inexpensively.

RED & GREEN SALAD WITH TOASTED ALMONDS
(Serves 6-8)

This is a great holiday salad. It's fast and very colorful. During a long Midwest winter, I crave greens and tomatoes from the garden. To me, these leaf lettuces and grape tomatoes have that fabulous out-of-the-garden taste. Thank God we can get them all year round.

1 small head each: red leaf lettuce, Boston lettuce and bibb lettuce, washed and broken into bite-size pieces
1 C. seedless cucumber, sliced
1 C. baby peas, if you're using frozen, just thaw them out first
1 C. celery, sliced
1 C. grape tomatoes, cut in half
1 red bell pepper, seeded and cut julienne
1 C. sliced almonds, lightly toasted

1.) Toss all salad ingredients together, except almonds, in a large salad bowl.
2.) Make Ginger Garlic Salad Dressing.

Ginger Garlic Salad Dressing:
1/2 C. grape seed oil*   1 t. grated ginger or 1/2 t. dry
1/4 C. rice wine vinegar   2 cloves garlic, minced
1 T. liquid aminos or soy sauce   A couple dashes of Louisiana Hot
2 t. honey   Sauce
2 t. sesame oil

3.) Put all the dressing ingredients in a jar with a lid. Shake well.
4.) Pour dressing on salad just before serving, toss and top with almonds.

170

*If you can't find grape seed oil, safflower would be fine.

****

Cucumbers are native to either Thailand or India, according to the general consensus of food historians. They have been cultivated in western Asia for at least 3,000 years. Emperors Augustus and Tiberius loved them so much, their imperial gardeners had to develop hothouse cultivation so they could be grown year round. It has been said Emperor Tiberius ate cucumbers, in the form of pickles, every single day.

Records of cucumber cultivation appear in France as early as the 9th Century. In 1494, the Spaniards introduced them in Haiti. The French explorer, Cartier, found very large cucumbers being grown in Montreal in 1535. They were really getting around by this time! When the first Europeans visited the Iroquois, cucumbers were being grown in native gardens.

Now here is an interesting little bit of information. During the 1600's a widespread prejudice developed against fresh fruits and vegetables. The majority of people felt summer diseases were caused by uncooked food. Cucumbers became known as "cowcumbers" because they were only fit to feed cows. Never mind the disease you could get if the cow picked up the dreaded summer disease from eating infected "cowcumbers" and you ate the meat from that cow. I guess the thinking process hadn't progressed that far.

Here are a couple folklore remedies cucumbers were at one time used for:

1.) Place a piece of cucumber skin on the forehead to ease the pain of a headache. I have no idea if this works.

2.) Eat the seeds to increase fertility. Hmmm. I don't know about this one either. Anybody tried either of these? Let me know.

Of course we know how soothing cool cucumber slices are over itchy, burning or just-plain-tired eyes. If you haven't tried this...go ahead...it works for me. Cut the slices thin so they stay on your eyes better. Now lay back and relax for 15 minutes. Ahhh! All better.

There's not much nutrition in cucumbers but they are a good alkaline vegetable if your body seems to lean toward the acidic side. One cup of cucumber only has 14 Calories. They do have a little Vitamin C, Calcium and Potassium. In the dead of winter, when I'm longing for green grass, I have some cucumber slices...all by themselves. They taste so fresh and green, it feels like spring can't be that far away.

ROASTED PEPPER, CHEESE SALAD
(Serves 6)

If you haven't tried roasting peppers before, it's really very easy. Roasting makes the flavor of the peppers simply explode! If you're crunched for time you can use the ones in a jar. I find them in the Italian aisle at the grocery store.

4 large red bell peppers, roasted* (directions below)
2 large green bell peppers, roasted
1 medium onion, thinly sliced
Olive oil
2 cloves garlic, crushed
1 1/2 C. corn, cut off the cob or frozen and thawed
1 C. celery, sliced
1 15oz. can black beans, drained and rinsed
1 C. chihuahua cheese, cut in cubes
1/3 C. fresh parsley or cilantro, your choice
Tiny sprinkle of salt
Freshly ground pepper
6-8 Boston lettuce leaves

Dressing:
2/3 C. safflower or grape seed oil
1/3 C. raspberry vinegar** (or rice wine vinegar)
1 t. salt
1 t. chili powder
1 t. cumin
1 t. oregano, dried
A couple drops of Louisiana Hot Sauce

*How to roast the peppers: Spray your broiler pan with cooking spray. Place peppers on broiler pan and broil until the skins are black, turning as each side chars. When the peppers are roasted all over, put them in a brown paper bag. Close it tightly and let them "sweat it out" for about 10 minutes. When cooled off, run them under cold water, while you peel the blackened skin off. The skins will slip off fairly easily. Remove the stems and seeds, then cut the peppers into strips. See, you really are getting to be quite a gourmet cook.

1.) While the peppers are roasting, stir fry the onions in a small amount of olive oil. When the onions begin to turn translucent, add the garlic and corn. Sauté for about 4 or 5 more minutes until the corn starts to get toasty. You'll need to stir this frequently so the garlic doesn't burn. Cool slightly.

2.) Put the sliced roasted peppers, onion, garlic, corn, celery, black beans, cheese and cilantro or parsley in a good-sized salad bowl.

3.) Make dressing and pour over salad. Marinate for at least 4 hours or overnight.

4.) Serve over a bed of the Boston lettuce leaves.

**Regarding raspberry vinegar: I tell you how to make it in the Tea and Other Diddies section at the back of the book if you are feeling adventurous or you cannot find it in your store. You can save a lot of money when you make your own. You can substitute rice wine vinegar. Regular white vinegar is too harsh for this recipe.

****

I love the taste of <u>cumin</u>. I consider it one of the sensuous herbs. It smells smokey, exotic and vibrant all at the same time. Cumin is an ancient herb that is even mentioned in the Bible. Native to the Mediterranean Sea area and

Egypt, Pliny the Elder, referred to it as the spice to make a student study better. Since it was so abundant during Roman times, it often replaced more expensive pepper. In fact, Christians used it as their tithe when they had no money. Hmm, I wonder if that would work today.

Saxons used cumin as a dry rub before roasting their peacocks and hens. During Medieval times it was hugely popular in Britain and most of Europe but somehow lost favor until Latin and Indian influence returned it to popularity again. It is one of the main spices in curry powder.

If you really want to bring out the flavor of cumin, toast it gently, in a frying pan, over medium-low heat, stirring constantly. The next time you make your famous chili, try toasting the cumin before you add it, whoa baby, that will make your taste buds dance!

OOOH BABY, BABY SALAD
(Serves 6)
Very tender and slightly sweet.

10 C. baby greens or a combination of your favorite leaf lettuce

1/4 C. sweet onion, sliced *very* thin, separate rings

1 C. jicama, peeled and cut julienne

1 1/2 C. fresh raspberries

1/2 C. black olives, sliced

Raspberry Vinaigrette:

1/2 C. safflower oil

1/4 C. raspberry vinegar, you can substitute rice wine vinegar

1 T. crushed fresh raspberries

1 T. honey

2 cloves garlic, crushed

1 t. dried savory or thyme (1 T. if you're using fresh)

1/2 t. salt

A couple grinds of fresh pepper

1.) Put all of the salad ingredients into a glass salad bowl...if you've got one. Other wise whatever you'd like.

2.) Make the dressing. Once you put the dressing on the salad you need to serve it immediately.

Wasn't this simple? The glass bowl makes it look very elegant and you hardly fussed at all.

Raspberries, to me, are one of the "fruits of the gods." I was in Denver once and had fresh raspberries with custard sauce for dessert. I thought I'd died and gone to heaven. Archeological evidence shows raspberries were gathered by humans long before its existence was recorded. In prehistoric times, raspberries spread all over Europe and Asia. If you've ever grown them in your yard, you know how quickly they can spread.

They are closely related to strawberries and are thought to be native to North America and Europe. The Roman naturalist, Pliny, wrote about people gathering raspberries near Mt. Ida in Greece. He strongly believed in their medicinal powers and it seems recent research would back up those beliefs. Raspberry leaf has been shown to lower blood sugar and is being studied by diabetic researchers. Traditionally it has been used to treat nausea and vomiting, particularly during pregnancy. It has also been used to prevent miscarriages, as a laxative and as a diuretic. There is nothing like raspberry leaf tea to ease those darn monthly cramps.

Herbalists consider the raspberry plant to be feminine. Its element is water and its powers are protection and love. Raspberry is a love-inducing food. (I'll go along with that.) Be careful not to keep raspberry too close to the bed. Being a pregnancy herb, it is likely to promote fertility in the bedroom.

Raspberries are packed with nutrition. They have lots of Calcium, both in the leaves (which is why they soothe cramps) and the berries. They have 8.4 g. of Fiber, 160 iu of Vitamin A, 32 mcg. Folic Acid and 187 mg. Potassium in one cup! That's one very impressive berry.

For you folks who like festivals, there's a wonderful one in Hopkins, Minnesota every year, in mid July. The first festival was held in 1934 and today the Hopkins Raspberry Festival is quite something. It's 10 days of fun and held in the prettiest little town you ever saw. In addition to the raspberries, it has a distinctive Main Street that you'll fall in love with. Check out their website and see if this is something you'd like to include in your travel plans. www.hopkinsraspberryfestival.com. Have a great time!!!

CRUNCHY, MUNCHY, FUN-CHY SALAD
(Serves 4-6)

This salad is loaded with fiber and fabulous taste. The Honey Curry Dressing is the perfect accompaniment. All of these ingredients are easy to find any time of the year.

10-12 C. romaine lettuce, torn into bite-sized pieces
1 C. radish sprouts or other fresh sprout
1 C. jicama, cut julienne
1 can sliced water chestnuts, cut julienne
1 C. celery, sliced
1 C. peapods, steam until tender crisp, then run under cold water
2 C. cooked turkey
1 C. toasted walnuts
2 Royal Gala apples, coarsely chopped
Juice from half a lemon

Honey Curry Dressing:
1 C. mayonnaise   1 1/2 T. honey
1 C. no fat sour cream   Milk to thin
1-2 T. curry powder   Salt and pepper to taste

1.) Go ahead and steam the peapods while you're preparing the rest of the salad ingredients. Just remember to keep an eye on those walnuts as they're toasting.
2.) Toss all the salad ingredients into the air...no, no...just kidding. Toss all the salad ingredients, except the apples, in a large bowl.
3.) In a small bowl, stir the lemon juice and the apples together. Add to the big salad bowl.

4.) For the dressing, whisk the mayonnaise and the sour cream together. Whisk in the curry powder and honey. Slowly whisk in enough milk to get the consistency you like. Taste. Add salt and pepper if you want.

5.) This makes a lot. Serve the dressing separately so each person can put on as much or as little as they want. You'll probably have some left over. It will keep for about a week. Hint: Honey Curry Dressing is excellent on poached salmon for another meal, later in the week.

****

Persian walnuts, English walnuts or black walnuts, which one of these do you have to run over with a car because their shells are so hard? Black walnuts! Have you ever tried to crack these guys open? A hammer works sometimes too. Today we are talking about Persian or English walnuts...same nut.

Walnuts have been around for millions of years! In fact, the walnut tree is thought to be the oldest tree food known to man. Legend has it that walnuts were one of the foods the wise men brought to baby Jesus. The oldest archeological site to find walnuts is in the Shanidar caves of northern Iraq. They were also found in a Mesolithic dunghill in Switzerland. Not exactly in Iraq's neighborhood. Walnuts were some of the effects found in Switzerland's lake district that dated as far back as the Stone Age or Neolithic Period (8,000-6,000 B.C.). These nuts have been around a very long time.

In ancient Persia, only royalty was allowed to eat them thus they were referred to as Royal Walnuts. King Solomon, of the Old Testament, is quoted as seeing, "the fruits of the valley" when he went down into the garden. The fruits were in reference to the abundant groves of walnuts. Around 2,000 B.C., in Mesopotamia, the Chaldeans left inscriptions on clay tablets revealing the existence of walnut groves in the famous Hanging Gardens of Babylon. The

Greeks and Romans dedicated them to their gods, Diana and Jupiter. In Pompeii, unshelled walnuts were among the foods found on the table at the Temple of Isis, on the fateful day that Mt. Vesuvius erupted.

The Romans brought them to England but they did not become part of the English food culture until after World War I, when they became a commercial enterprise. However, in France the walnut was so popular, the French peasants were expected to tithe walnuts to the church.

Today, California's walnut industry, in Stockton, produces 99% of the U.S.'s commercial supply and 2/3 of the world's!! WOW! The first commercial walnut groves began in Goleta, California in 1867 but later moved to central California's "perfect walnut-growing conditions."

Walnuts are considered to be one of the most nutritious nuts around. They are full of Vitamin E, Calcium, Copper, Magnesium, Phosphorus and Potassium. There are also studies being done pertaining to the walnut's ability to lower bad cholesterol. Keep your eyes and ears peeled for future studies on the health benefits of walnuts.

CRAB LOUIE OBISPO
(Serves 4)

This is based on my Grandma Nicol's recipe. When we were little, my grandparents used to take us to a place called Nelscott, somewhere along the Oregon coast line. It's not named that anymore, it's called Lincoln City. I doubt if I would recognize it, but I still have all the memories. If you luuuuv crab like I do, you will love this recipe. You could easily substitute shrimp for the crab if you wanted to.

Salad:
2 C. lump crabmeat, try not to use canned and DO NOT use that fake stuff
7 C. shredded red leaf lettuce
1 C. grape tomatoes, sliced in half
1 C. baby peas, thawed if you're using frozen
1 C. celery, thinly sliced
2 hard boiled eggs, chopped
1/2 C. green or black olives or a combination of both

You can use the *New Dawn Dressing*, below, or your favorite Thousand Island Dressing, like my Grandma did.

1.) Put all of the salad ingredients in a large bowl and toss gently so you don't pulverized the crabmeat.
2.) Make the dressing.

New Dawn Salad Dressing:

2/3 C. mayonnaise

2/3 C. no fat sour cream

3 T. ketchup

2 T. milk

1 t. Worcestershire sauce

1 1/2 t. dehydrated minced onion

1/2 T. dried parsley

1/4 t. garlic powder

2 T. dill pickle, finely diced

3-5 shakes Louisiana Hot Sauce, more if desired

3.) Whisk all of the dressing ingredients together and let sit for at least 15 minutes.

4.) Serve dressing separately so each person can put on what they want.

****

You're going to pass out when I tell you this story. While my family and I were staying at Nelscott, Grandma would get up early every morning. Sometimes I'd go with her down to the crab shack to get the crabmeat for her Crab Louie, which was usually for lunch. I'd run along beside her, playing tag with the waves of the Pacific Ocean, while she walked, partly bent over, so she could check out any treasures the ocean might have washed up during the night. Nine times out of ten, she'd find an unusual agate or a fabulous shell or sometimes even a hand blown glass ball that Japanese fishermen used in their fishing nets. Whenever she found one of those, I would marvel at the fact that this fragile glass ball crossed the ocean from Japan to the wild Oregon coast, in tact. If that little ball could talk, what adventures it must have had.

The crab shack was right on the beach. After my Grandma and I had finished looking for rocks and shells, we'd march up to that fishy smelling little hut. My Grandma would plunk down her dollar and get one pound of the freshest crabmeat you ever tasted. That's right...ONE DOLLAR!! We'd stroll back to where we were staying, satisfied and happy in the knowledge that we were going to have the best and freshest Crab Louie anyone had ever eaten. Honestly, I felt like the luckiest person on the globe. I love those memories. Thanks, Grandma.

Now on to the facts. There are over 4,000 varieties of edible crab around the world. John Hay, American diplomat and journalist was quoted to say, "There are three species of creatures who when they seem coming, are going and when they seem going, are coming: diplomats, women and crabs." Next to shrimp, crab is the most popular crustacean in the United States. There is a species of Japanese giant crab that can measure 12 1/2 feet across, and the Tasmanian giant crab can weigh as much as 30 pounds!

Crabs are one of the oldest species on Earth, dating back over 200 million years. They are literally a living fossil. Evidence shows that crab and lobster have been fished since the Stone Age.

Nutritionally, they are an excellent source of Chromium, which works with insulin to metabolize sugar, and helps to raise good cholesterol (HDL) levels, which can aid in reducing the risk of heart disease and stroke. Three ounces of crab only have 71 Calories. It also has lots of Calcium, Phosphorus, Potassium and Magnesium. If you haven't had crab in a while and you love it, isn't it about time you had it again?

TOMATO CORN SALAD with HONEY LIME DRESSING
(Serves 2)

This is such a beautiful salad for a hot sticky night. Cool and refreshing, the dressing glides over your taste buds and gives you just the slightest bite. This recipe is very easily doubled.

Salad:
1 C. corn, fresh or frozen and thawed
1 avocado, chopped
1 large tomato, chopped
1/3 C. sliced black olives

Pinch of salt
1/4 C. sweet onion, chopped
3 T. cilantro, slivered
Fresh ground pepper
Red leaf lettuce

Honey Lime Dressing:
1/4 c. safflower oil
1 T. liquid aminos
2 t. honey

1/8 t. cumin, just a touch
1-2 T. fresh lime juice
2 cloves crushed garlic

1.) Gently mix all the salad ingredients, except the red leaf lettuce, in a salad bowl.
2.) Put all of the dressing ingredients in a jar with a lid. Shake well, then pour over salad.
3.) Chill for at least one hour. This is one salad where the flavors have to get to know each other for a while.
4.) Serve on red leaf lettuce. Very pretty presentation.

One of my favorite summertime drinks is homemade limeade with lots of ice. I don't care if it's made with the smaller, key limes or the bigger ones. My Mom used to make it more on the tart side...not too sweet. I love it that way!!!

Limes have been cultivated for thousands of years. Limes are native to the tropical regions of Asia or India and are the smallest member of the citrus family. The history of the lemon and the lime are intertwined because early reference to citrus does not distinguish one from the other.

During Columbus' second voyage in 1493, he stopped at the Canary Islands and obtained lime seeds, as well as seeds from other fruits and vegetables. He planted lime seeds on what is now Haiti. Later, Spanish conquistadores took limes from those groves and planted them in St. Augustine, Florida. That's how limes got to America...global cooperation!

In my research on limes, I discovered where the term "limey" comes from. Scurvy, a disease causing severe anemia, used to be the scourge of the British navy until Scottish naval surgeon, Sir James Lind, discovered scurvy was caused by lack of Vitamin C. Knowing limes were loaded with Vitamin C and were also plentiful, Sir James prescribed daily doses of lime juice to stop scurvy in it's tracks. Over one and a half million gallons of lime juice were consumed between 1795-1815, to reduce the scurvy mortality rate of British seamen.

The two kinds of limes I researched are the larger Persian variety (the kind you usually find in your local grocery store) and Key limes, which are much smaller, but are the limes used in the original recipe for Key Lime Pie. Florida used to be the largest grower of key limes until Hurricane Andrew demolished the groves in 1992. Today Mexico is the largest producer of Key limes, while Florida decided to change to the larger Persian limes.

186

One tablespoon of lime juice contains a whopping 4.5mg of Vitamin C, even more than a tablespoon of lemon juice (3.8). Another little tidbit: fresh lime juice can bring soothing relief if you happen to run into stinging coral.

WE ARE LIVING IN A WORLD WHERE
LEMONADE IS MADE FROM ARTIFICIAL
FLAVORS AND FURNITURE POLISH IS
MADE FROM REAL LEMONS.

-Alfred E. Newman

NORTHERN LIGHTS SALAD
(Serves 6-8)

This is a make ahead salad. The Herb-y Orange Dressing needs to "marry" the salad ingredients for at least 4 hours. The wild rice with the fruit, the mint and the toasted nuts is such an unexpected combination. Your taste buds will go wild.

1 1/2 C. wild rice

2 C. water

1 t. salt

1 1/2 C. vegetable broth

1 C. dried, sweetened cranberries

1 6 oz. can crushed pineapple, do not drain

2/3 C. finely chopped, sweet onion

3 T. fresh mint, chopped

1 C. toasted pecans or macadamia nuts

Herb-y Orange Dressing:

1/3 C. safflower oil

3 T. honey

1/2 t. dry tarragon

a couple grinds of fresh pepper

1/2 C. orange juice

2 cloves garlic, crushed

1/2 t. salt

1.) Cook wild rice in water, vegetable broth and salt for one hour, or until rice is cooked thoroughly and not too chewy. Cool for about half an hour, stirring once in a while.

2.) Put all the dressing ingredients in a jar with a lid. Shake well and set aside.

3.) Meanwhile, in a large bowl, combine cranberries, pineapple and sweet onion.

4.) Toast the nuts, in a large frying pan, over low heat, stirring constantly, until they're nice and crunchy and fragrant...it usually takes about five to seven minutes. Set them aside. They will be added just before you serve.

5.) Add the cooled wild rice, mint and dressing to the cranberry mixture. Mix well. Refrigerate for AT LEAST 4 HOURS. Don't forget to add the nuts just before you serve...you want them nice and crunchy.

This salad is dedicated to Minnesota, where wild rice is abundant and the people are some of the warmest, friendliest folks you'll ever meet. I was way up in the Boundary Waters Canoe Area, when I saw my first incredible display of Northern Lights... Heaven's fireworks. It's a goose bump memory!

****

For hundreds of years wild rice has been a diet staple of the Great Lakes Indian tribes. Five hundred years ago, the Chippewa (Ojibawas) were the largest tribe in the northeastern portion of America, with a population of about 50,000. Wild rice was one of the main foods in their diet. The Menominee of Wisconsin, take their name from the Indian word for wild rice, menomin, which means, "good berry."

Wild rice is actually a type of wild water grass, whose seeds are cooked and eaten like rice. Even though it's found in most states east of the Rockies...Michigan, Wisconsin and Minnesota produce almost 2/3 of the world's supply. There is a variety that is found in Manchuria, Korea, Burma and northeastern India but it is very different than what we are used to.

In the early 1800's, a bushel of wild rice sold for $1.50. In the late 1940's a pound cost somewhere between 30-40 cents. Compare that to the $5.00-$10.00 a pound today. However, the harvest of wild rice, especially from public waters, is still done by hand and is very labor intensive. If you're ever in northeastern Minnesota, driving on Highway 61 along the shore of Lake Superior, you'll see little homemade stands selling wonderful Minnesota wild rice, at a very reasonable price. Isn't it time for a ROAD TRIP?

Americans love wild rice. Annual production in the 1940's was around 200,000 pounds, compared to that of today...over 1,500,000 pounds. We must know something. Not only do we love its taste, wild rice is extremely nutritious. It is high in Protein, low in Fat, and is an excellent source of Potassium(683mg.), Phosphorus (693mg.) and B Vitamins. One half cup of wild rice contains 9.9g of fiber compared to 6.5g in the same amount of brown rice.

You're going to love this recipe...I just know you will. Get creative and add some of your own touches to it. If you're anything like me, experiment...experiment... experiment.

IT'S NOT YOUR CIRCUMSTANCES
THAT MAKE OR BREAK YOUR DAY.
IT'S YOUR ATTITUDE.

-Evangeline Lilly

BLUSHING RICE SALAD
(Serves 6)

This is a beautiful, simple salad. The flavors are even better two or three days later. My friends all rave about the taste and how easy it is to make.

6 C. cooked rice (I use half basmati and half brown rice)
1 t. salt
splash of olive oil
1 15 oz. can diced <u>tomatoes</u>, this makes the blush
3 stalks celery, chopped
1/2 c. black olives, sliced
1 green pepper, chopped
2 T. Parmesan cheese
1 T. fresh parsley, chopped

Mustard Garlic Dressing:
1/2 C. mayonnaise
1/2 C. fat free sour cream
1 1/2 t. honey mustard
1 t. honey
3 cloves garlic, crushed
1 t. dried basil
2 T. milk
A couple grinds black pepper
A bit of sea salt (optional)

1.) Cook rice with the teaspoon of salt and the splash of olive oil. Cool rice slightly.

191

2.) Toss rice, tomatoes with the juice, celery, olives, green pepper and Parmesan cheese together in a bowl.

3.) Whisk all the dressing ingredients together. If you like a thinner dressing, add a little more milk. Chill for one hour.

To the world, you might be one person, but to one person, you might be the world.

There's nothing like home grown <u>tomatoes</u>. This year we are growing only heirloom tomatoes. We've got Black Krim and Black Prince, both black tomatoes from Siberia; a Lemon Tomato; Evergreen, which are bright green when they're ripe; Brandywine, sort of heart-shaped and pink; and the very red Arkansas Traveler. Can you see all of these in a tomato salad dressed only in a vinaigrette? It will be a veritable rainbow!

Peru is where tomatoes originated. Eight species are known to grow wild there still. Peruvians gathered them in the wild instead of cultivating them. At that time they were only about the size of what we know as cherry tomatoes today. They got as far north as Mexico before the Europeans arrived. Tomatoes traveled back to Spain with the conquistadors, like so many other fruits and vegetables. Italians became passionate about them. The Italian word pomodoro "apple of love" or "golden apple" refers to the first variety to reach Europe, which was yellow.

Because botanists recognized the tomato to be in the same family as belladonna and nightshade, much of northern Europe considered them poisonous. Thomas Jefferson, who was raising tomatoes by 1782, was one of the few who thought otherwise. It wasn't until the early 20th Century that Europeans changed their minds and started eating them. Directions in a turn-of-the-century American cookbook, stated, "tomatoes must be cooked for at least three hours or else they will not lose their raw taste."

Is the tomato a fruit or a vegetable? That is the question. Botanically speaking it is a fruit but from a culinary point of view, it is generally used as a vegetable. It might interest you to know that the Supreme Court ruled on this very subject in 1893. The Court was ruling on this business, in the first place, for tariff purposes. The Court rejected the botanical truth even though the tomato is actually a huge berry, and categorized it a vegetable. So it could be taxed, of course.

In warmer regions tomato plants are perennial and flower regardless of the length of the day. When I was in Kauai one January, we were driving around a little neighborhood (because we were lost). Every yard had huge tomato plants growing and I mean huge. This was quite a novelty to someone born and raised in the Midwest.

One medium-sized tomato has only 24 Calories, 766iu of Vitamin A, 254mg. Potassium, is very low in Sodium, and has no Fat. I can't wait until my tomatoes are ripe. Yummy!

BIG, HAPPY FAMILY SALAD
(Serves 4-6)

This is another make-ahead salad. The dressing acts as a marinade to bring all the flavors together into one big, happy family. The longer it takes for the ingredients to get acquainted, the better the taste.

Salad:

2 cans chick peas, drained   1 C. celery, sliced

1 medium tomato, cubed   1 C. Chihuahua cheese, cubed

1/2 C. black olives, sliced   2 T. cilantro, chopped

1 T. fresh parsley, chopped   5 C. baby lettuces

Marinating dressing:

3 cloves garlic, crushed   1/3 C. olive oil

1/4 C. red wine vinegar   1 t. cumin

1/2 t. dried oregano   1 t. salt

A couple grinds of fresh pepper

1.) Mix salad ingredients together, except for the lettuces, in a medium-sized bowl.

2.) Put all the dressing ingredients in a jar with a lid. Shake well. Pour dressing over salad, then marinate for at least 2 hours.

3.) When you're ready to serve, place a nice handful of the lettuces on individual salad plates. Top with the bean mixture. Serve immediately. You can garnish with additional cilantro, parsley or sliced black olives if you want to.

4.) This serves 4-6 depending on whether or not you are using this as the main course or a side dish. It's a wonderful salad full of color and textures. Your tongue and your tummy will be very happy. Do I hear tango music?

THE ONLY WAY TO HAVE A FRIEND IS TO BE ONE.
-Ralph Waldo Emerson

Vinegar is actually wine or a liquid that has gone bad. The English word comes from the French word, vin which means wine and aigre, which translates to sour...and it is that, sour. It's the other components ie., red wine, apple cider, rice wine, and so on, which give each variety its individual taste.

It has a very long history. Traces of vinegar have been found in 10,000 year old Egyptian pottery. I remember from my Sunday school class, learning that Jesus was offered a "drink" from a sponge soaked in wine vinegar, just before he died. I always thought that was horribly cruel until, in my research, I discovered Caesar's armies drank diluted vinegar for a thirst-quenching drink. Hmmm. The soldiers also used it for cleaning wounds and cleansing the body. The Roman upper class would dip small pieces of bread in it between courses to cleanse the palate. During the 10th Century, vinegar's uses expanded to cleaning contaminated objects and to purify the air during plagues.

Today, a good quality apple cider vinegar is excellent for a lot of what ails you. If you mix 2 teaspoons in 6 oz. of water (you can add a little honey if you need to) and drink it, this little concoction, used on a regular basis, can help arthritis pain, clean out the arteries, help with memory, aid in burning fat and a bunch of other things. I use Bragg's Apple Cider Vinegar, which is now available at my grocery store. Through them, you can order a book that explains ALL its health benefits.

I want to take some time to address the interesting subject of balsamic vinegar. I personally, love it's full, rich flavor. The true "aceto balsamico" is seldom available. The officially approved substitute, which must be at least 12 years old, sells for a small fortune...over $100.00 for a 3.3 oz. bottle!!! The REAL "aceto balsamico" is only produced in Northern Italy and has been made since the 11th Century. Until recently it was only produced for family use, with barrels passed down from one generation to the next. This inherited balsamic vinegar has often been aged from 50-200 years! Can you imagine it's history?! Less expensive, industrialized versions are now widely available in a variety of price ranges.

Check out the helpful little section, Tea and Other Diddies, toward the back of the book on how it make your own flavored vinegars. It's easy and makes a great gift to give to yourself or some other special individual, especially if you use fruit or herbs you grew with your own two hands.

THROW TOGETHER SALAD
(Serves 4~6)

Make this salad ahead of time so the flavors can get to know each other. This is such an easy dish to make. The combination of ingredients will knock your socks off. Serve it with a crusty loaf of Italian bread and you're all set.

2 heads of roasted garlic
1 C. black olives
1 C. celery, sliced
1 pint grape tomatoes
4 green onions, sliced
8 oz. of your favorite Italian salad dressing
Fresh ground black pepper to taste

8 oz. fresh mozzarella
1 C. green olives
½ C. roasted red peppers, chopped
¼ C. fresh basil, cut julienne

Shopping hint: When you buy the ingredients for this you have options...quite a few actually. Fresh mozzarella comes in large balls, little balls, logs and sometimes you can find it braided. Occasionally you can find it marinated. Now don't get excited or confused. Relax. Pick whatever you like. As for the olives, what kind do you like? Get a couple different black and a couple different green...or use olives right out of the can or jar. It'll taste great. Just remember to remove any pits. Also, you can find roasted red peppers in jars next to the olives. This will save you time. Make sure you drain the liquid off.

1.) Preheat your oven to 350 degrees to roast the garlic. Peel some of the outside papery skin off. Cut a little bit off the top off each head. (Just so you can see the tips of some of the cloves.) Put in a baking pan, drizzle with olive oil and sprinkle with a tiny bit of salt. Bake for 30-45 minutes depending on the size of your garlic heads. They will be done when you pierce a clove and the knife goes in easily.

2.) While the garlic is roasting, cut the mozzarella into bite-sized pieces. Throw the cheese, olives, celery, roasted peppers, tomatoes, green onions, and basil into a large bowl. Pour the dressing over. Add a couple grinds of black pepper. Mix gently.

3.) When the garlic is done you have a couple options again. After it's cooled slightly, you can pop the individual cloves out and put them in the salad or you can squeeze the garlic out into the salad. Squeezing it will break it up so it melts into the salad more. I've done it both ways. Either way is fine, it just depends on how you feel...whole or smushed? Hmmmmmm! Chill for 2-3 hours.

****

Most of my research indicated the origin of olives was in the Mediterranean area. Olive trees, oldest known cultivated trees in the world, were around before written language was invented. Recent archeological discoveries prove that wild olive trees existed during the Neolithic Period (3,500-5,000 B.C.) It is known that the Phoenicians took olive trees to the shores of Africa and southern Europe around the time of the Minoan civilization. The olive trees on the Mount of Olives, in Jerusalem, are thought to be over 2,000 years old.

There is a wonderful Greek myth, involving the olive that is always fun to tell. Pull up a seat. Once upon a time there was a great contest between Athena and Poseidon. The prize was to be the property of Athens and most of the Attica region. Ahhh, you are probably saying to yourself...a very rich prize indeed. Anyway, the judge of this event was Zeus, himself. The winner would be the one who created the greatest, and most useful, new wonder. Poseidon created a new animal, the horse. Athena created a new tree, the olive tree. Zeus decided the horse was for war and the olive was for peace. Athena won. Now you know where extending the olive branch, as a sign of peace, comes from.

The olive tree has been manipulated by humans for thousands of years. It's hard to tell which variety comes from which. Shrub-like wild olives can still be found in the Middle East. They are the original stock from which all other olives are descended. There really aren't different "kinds" of olives. They're just the same basic type, picked at different stages of ripeness and cured in a variety of ways. Green olives are the unripe fruit of the olive tree. All fresh olives are bitter and tough. If you see one on a tree in California and decide to pop one in your mouth, you're in for a big surprise.

Most of you know how good olive oil is for you so it stands to reason that olives are good for you too. They are loaded with monosaturates, which is a good Fat. They also contain polyphenols which are believed to ward off cancer. Olives also contain modest amounts of Calcium and Vitamin A. One large black olive contains 7 Calories. The down side is they are high in Sodium so if you are watching your salt intake go easy on the olives. I had some large green olives not too long ago, that were stuffed with blue cheese. Ooooh! They are now my new olive favorites.

The discovery of a new dish
does more for human happiness
than the discovery of a new star.

-Brillat-Savarin

GARLIC CILANTRO DRESSING
(Makes 1 3/4 C.)

This little recipe stands on it's own. It has no particular salad it goes with because it goes with so many things. I played around with it one afternoon and was so pleased with the results I decided to include it in the book. If you hate cilantro you can use parsley or dill. This is also an excellent topping for red snapper, sea scallops, or baked potatoes. Actually it's also fabulous on tomatoes fresh from the garden. It's a pretty good veggie dip too.

2/3 C. mayonnaise

1/3 C. milk

3 cloves garlic, crushed

1-2 T. fresh cilantro, chopped

A tiny sprinkle of salt

2/3 C. no fat sour cream

1 1/2 T. fresh lime juice

1/2 t. allspice

A couple grinds fresh pepper

1.) Whisk all the ingredients together until the dressing is smooth.

2.) Chill for at least an hour. Voila!

****

Some food historians believe an olive oil/egg mixture can be traced back to Roman or Egyptian times, that could be the original mayonnaise. Mayonnaise is a partial emulsion of oil and egg with vinegar or lemon juice and salt, sometimes seasoned with sugar and various spices. (Trader Joe's sells a wonderful mayo without sugar, in case you're interested.) You just put all those ingredients in a blender or food processor, whirl them around...mayo. A lot of people are afraid of homemade mayonnaise these days because it's made with raw eggs. However, if you know the source of your eggs and you keep it refrigerated...well, homemade is always the best.

The mayonnaise we are familiar with was developed in France. It seems the chef of the Duke of Richelieu was making a victory dinner for his boss. While the duke was in a battle with the British at Fort Mahon, the chef was making a sauce made from cream and eggs when he realized he had no cream...boy, does that sound familiar? He decided to substitute olive oil. The sauce was named Mahonnaise in honor of the duke's victory at Fort Mahon.

Here's a little historical tidbit you might be interested in. It seems the duke was known for the strange habit of inviting his dinner guests to dine in the buff. I guess he wanted to make sure no one ran off with the silverware. Tee-hee.

Mahonnaise became mayonnaise through a printing error and it stuck. Early French immigrants who lived in Fort Mahon, brought the original recipe to America, where they ended up settling in Minnesota. In 1905, Richard Hellman opened a delicatessen in New York City which featured salads his wife made. The mayonnaise she used in these salads became so popular, he started selling it separately.

I tend to be a food purist. I like the food I'm putting in my body to be as close to its natural state as possible. Rather than use all that low fat, no fat mayonnaise out there that contains ingredients with 26 letters, I'd prefer the real thing cut with all natural no-fat sour cream. Let's face it, those substitutes don't taste anything like the original...who are they kidding?

Scuse me...I had to run down to get a jar of Trader Joe's Mayonnaise to check out the nutritional facts. Just as I thought: 1 T. has 100 Calories, 12g of Fat, 5mg Cholesterol, 70 mg Sodium but NO SUGAR. So those of you doing the low carb thing...here's your mayo.

Chapter 7

Soups

Woo-hoo!

MERLIN'S MAGICAL MUSHROOM MEDLEY
(Makes 6-8 servings)

I developed this recipe based on a canned soup named Scotch Broth that my Mom used to serve when I was little. When I was finished creating the recipe, the only resemblance to the original was that it has barley and carrots. This is such a cozy soup, you will probably want to put on your favorite slippers as you prepare it.

3 T. olive oil

1 C. each, chopped carrots, onion & celery

3-5 cloves garlic, crushed

1 lb. fresh white mushrooms, sliced

½ lb. fresh shitaki mushrooms, stems removed and discarded, tops sliced

8 C. vegetable or chicken broth

1 T. fresh marjoram or 1 t. dry

1 T. fresh rosemary, chopped fine or 1 t. dry, crumbled

1 C. barley

4 T. cornstarch

½ C. water

2 C. whole milk

1 ½ C. grated mozzarella cheese

Salt & pepper to taste

1.) In a large stock pot, sauté the carrots, onions, celery, garlic and a bit of salt and pepper in the olive oil for 5-10 minutes, stirring frequently.

2.) Add the sliced mushrooms and continue to sauté for 5 more minutes. Take a whiff...inhale...doesn't it smell wonderful?

3.) Next add broth, marjoram, rosemary and barley. Bring to a boil, lower the heat, and simmer, covered for 30-45 minutes (some barley is very tiny so it will cook faster) or until barley is tender.

4.) Mix cornstarch with the ½ C. water. Bring soup up to a low boil and slowly stir cornstarch/water mixture into the soup, stirring constantly (if you don't, you'll get lumps).

5.) Lower the heat, stir in the milk and 1 C. of the mozzarella cheese. Add salt and pepper to taste.

6.) Heat thoroughly but do not bring to a boil. Ladle soup into bowls and top with remaining cheese.   Ahhhhhh!

****

Garlic is the featured ingredient in this recipe. I could write a whole book on the wonder of garlic but that's already been done. Check out the book, The Healing Benefits of Garlic, by John Heinerman, Ph.D. Before I continue, you need to know my own little garlic story.

About 9 years ago, I developed a case of shingles. Any of you out there who've had shingles know how horribly painful they are. It hurts to wear your clothes. OW! In a book I have called, Miracle Medicine Foods, by Rex Adams, there was a case about a lady who cured her shingles by eating lots of garlic. So I roasted 40 cloves of garlic and ate them. The next morning my shingles were gone!!!! I swear! My kids wouldn't sit next to me in church, in fact no one did, but I could wear clothes. It was so worth it.

OK, now on to some of the information I discovered. Garlic was once thought to possess magical powers against evil. Odysseus used it to keep the sorceress Circe, from turning him into a pig. That's a very useful bit of information, don't you think? The Egyptians used to swear on a clove of garlic when they took any solemn oath. Romans took it to strengthen them in battle, since it was the herb of Mars, the Roman god of war. In this country,

206

Indians used wild garlic in cooking and as medicine, since their recorded history.

Medicinally, garlic has been prescribed since biblical times. In the Far East, ancient herbalists used it to treat high blood pressure, as some herbalists do today. Recent findings show garlic is good for infections. One of garlic's components, allicin, has antibacterial action equal to that of 1% penicillin! Herbalists have also traditionally used garlic to rid pets and people of worms and parasites, relieve congestion, inhibit blood clotting, and lower cholesterol. What an herb!!!

Have YOU had your garlic today???

LIVE EACH DAY IN A CONSCIOUS WAY, INSTEAD OF UNCONSCIOUS AND AFRAID.

HAPPY SOUP
(Serves 4-6)

This soup is so colorful and tasty PLUS it's quick and simple. How much more could you want from a soup? It'll also make you feel all warm and cuddly which is bound to put a big grin on your face.

2 T. olive oil

1 lg. onion, chopped

7 cloves of garlic, crushed

1 # fresh spinach

1 C. corn, fresh or frozen

1 C. zucchini, grated

1 C. carrot, grated

1 can dark, red kidney beans

2 qts veggie or chicken stock

1-2 t. dry tarragon

Salt & pepper to taste

Parmesan cheese, divided

3 C. cooked brown rice or couscous

Maybe a little or a lot grated mozzarella cheese

1.) Make the rice or couscous according to package directions. That can be cooking while you make the soup.

2.) Sauté the onion and garlic in the olive oil for 2-3 minutes, stirring constantly so the garlic doesn't burn. Make sure the spinach is well washed, then add it to the onions and garlic. Continue to sauté for another 3-4 minutes.

3.) Next add corn, zucchini, and carrots. Continue to sauté for another couple of minutes, stirring frequently.

4.) Add kidney beans, stock, tarragon, 2 T. of grated parmesan cheese...salt and pepper to taste.

5.) Cover and simmer over low heat for 10 minutes.

6.) To serve, put 1/2 C. of the brown rice or couscous in the bottom of a soup bowl. Cover with Happy Soup and top with some parmesan cheese.*

*Sometimes I use grated mozzarella to top the soup instead. We don't mind having mozzarella strings hanging from our chins. It depends on your moooood. How playful are you today?

****

Tarragon is the key to the flavor of this recipe. It's name comes from the French word *esdragon* meaning "little dragon." The dragon-like roots may strangle the plant if not divided often. Pliny, the Roman scholar said it could prevent fatigue. People of the Middle Ages used to put it in their shoes before they went on long foot trips to keep their feet happy. Thomas Jefferson was an early distributor of tarragon in the newly-formed United States. He grew it in his gardens and distributed it freely.

Tarragon is mostly considered a culinary herb but it does have medicinal capabilities. It has been used to simulate the appetite, relieve gas and colic, and cure rheumatism. There is no scientific backup to this, but it appears tarragon can protect food as an antioxidant. It may also be useful as an anti-fungal as well.

Be careful when using this herb in any recipe. It is very powerful and can overshadow other flavors. Some people like a stronger tarragon flavor, some don't. I think of it as an elegant herb. To me it has such a rich, classy flavor. It's wonderful sprinkled on fish, potatoes (add it to your favorite mashed potato recipe), tomatoes, cauliflower or asparagus. Just go easy. Also don't add it until the last 10 minutes of cooking. It might get a little bitter if it's cooked too long.

It makes a wonderful flavored vinegar. Just put 5-6 sprigs of tarragon in a sterilized bottle, fill with white vinegar, and cork. Set the bottle in a dark place for two weeks to allow the tarragon to infuse the vinegar. Tarragon vinegar makes a wonderful gift, maybe with a raffia bow, and a salad dressing recipe or two. Imagine how special someone would feel receiving such a gift...especially if you grew the tarragon yourself. It's easy to grow. Other plants love it because it boosts their growth.

EVERY AUTUMN, WHEN THE WIND TURNS COLD AND DARKNESS COMES EARLY, I AM SUDDENLY HAPPY. IT'S TIME TO START MAKING SOUP AGAIN

.-Leslie Newman

POTATO MUSHROOM POTAGE
(Serves 6-8)

My note to you...PLEASE read all the directions through first. It is not really a complicated soup but there are steps you need to follow or your Potage (pronounced po taj) might end up a mish mosh. This is an aromatic soup whose fragrance will transport you to a cozy, country bistro in France.

3 T. <u>olive oil</u>, divided
1 C. celery, chopped
1 head garlic, peeled & crushed
2 C. potatoes, peeled & cubed
3 C. cooked chicken or turkey
¼ C. white wine, optional
**Crème fraiche or sour cream

1 C. onion, chopped
1 C. chopped carrots
4 C. chicken stock
8 oz. baby portabellas, sliced
*2 t. Herbs de Provence
Salt and Pepper to taste

*Note: If you can't find Herbs de Provence you can use crushed rosemary.
**Crème fraiche is located near the cheese or sour cream in your grocery store.

1.) In a large pot, sauté onion, celery, and carrots in 2 T. olive oil, until onions start to get a golden brown around the edges. Now put in the garlic and stir for a few minutes over low heat making sure the garlic doesn't burn.

2.) Add your broth and potato cubes. Cover and simmer for about 15 minutes. This is the soup base.

3.) While the potatoes are cooking, sauté your mushrooms in a frying pan, using the remaining 1 T. olive oil. Also get out a large bowl or pot and your food processor or blender. You are about to do something very exciting with the veggies that are simmering away.

211

4.) OK...this is when it can get a little tricky if you decide to fall asleep at the "wheel" so to speak. Do not add the mushrooms to your onion-celery-carrot-potato mixture. You are going to <u>carefully</u> puree the soup base AND THEN add the rest of the ingredients.

5.) Ready? All righty then, puree <u>small</u> amounts of the soup base. When one batch is pureed, put it in the large bowl or pot I told you to get out in Step #3. Be careful! Remember this is hot, so do small amounts at a time. Otherwise, you will have hot puree all over your counter and yourself and that is no fun.

6.) I know the pureeing part is a bit of a challenge but the end result is sooooo worth it. You'll probably start to puree other soups in your recipe collection...just for the sake of the end result. Just go slow and be careful...you'll do just fine.

7.) Once the soup base is pureed, put it back into the original soup pot. Turn the heat on low and add the sautéed mushrooms, chicken or turkey, white wine if you want, Herbs de Provence or rosemary, and salt and freshly ground pepper to taste. Heat everything thoroughly. It should take about 10 minutes. Can you believe how fabulous this smells?

8.) Serve immediately with a dollop of crème fraiche or sour cream. Close your eyes and pretend you are on a romantic balcony in the French Alps with Mont Blanc right before your eyes. Ahhhh! Bon appetite!

****

Fossilized remains of olive trees were found near Livorno, Italy dating from 20 million years ago! Archeologists were excavating in the strata of a volcano's crater in Greece and found perfectly fossilized olive leaves dating back 50-60,000 years. The olive seems to be one of the oldest plants that still exists on the Earth today. Many origins of its cultivation are claimed but most of my sources agree olive tree cultivation began around 5,000 B.C. around Crete, then spread to Syria, Palestine and Israel. A few of those sources state cultivation could be much older than that. Greece, in particular Mycenae, was the hub of olive cultivation until 1500 B.C.

Homer called <u>olive oil</u>, "liquid gold." Ancient Greek athletes rubbed it all over their bodies to retain body heat. The oil was considered medicinal as well as magical. In Egypt, Greece and Rome olive oil was infused with flowers, herbs and grasses to produce medicine as well as cosmetics. In a dig in Mycenae, a tablet was found listing fennel, sesame, celery, mint, sage, watercress, rose and juniper as just some of the herbs used to prepare olive oil ointments and medicines.

The olive tree is a symbol of abundance, glory and peace. I'm sure you've heard of "extending an olive branch" as a sign for peace. Olive branch crowns were emblems of benediction and purification. They were ritually offered to deities and powerful figures.

Extra virgin olive oil is the most digestible of edible Fats. It helps to assimilate Vitamins A, D and K, as well as containing essential acids that our bodies cannot produce. It is also known to slow down aging and help bile, liver and intestinal function. Hail to "liquid gold."

TOO GOOD TO BE TRUE SOUP
(Serves 6-8)

A good stock is the key to this absolutely fabulous, wonderful, superb soup. (If I do say so myself.) If you have turkey or chicken bones hanging around from another recipe or after Thanksgiving dinner, use those to make a nice homemade stock. One time I made this using stock we'd cooked up from a smoked turkey. Yum!!

6 C. chicken, turkey or vegetable stock, preferably homemade
3 C. cooked and mashed <u>sweet potatoes</u> or you can use butternut squash too
(this is a good way to use leftovers)
1 T. butter
1/3 C. brown sugar, not packed
4 slices turkey bacon
¼ C. dry white wine, optional
1 C. water
3 C. uncooked rotini
1 T. fresh marjoram or 1 ½ t. dry
Salt and Pepper to taste

1.) If you're using leftover sweet potatoes or squash, you can skip this step. First thing you need to do is cook the sweet potatoes or butternut squash in 3/4 C. water until tender. Drain most of the water, add butter and brown sugar, mash together.

2.) Meanwhile, bake turkey bacon at 400 degrees for 10 minutes. Pat any extra fat off with a paper towel. Chop up into small pieces.

3.) While turkey bacon is in the oven, bring stock to a boil in a large pot. Reduce heat, add cooked sweet potatoes or squash and turkey bacon (it will be done by this time). Stir until well blended.

4.) Add wine, the 1 C. of water and the rotini. Bring to a low boil, stirring occasionally.

5.) Cook, covered, over low heat, until pasta is very tender. This usually takes about 25 minutes.

6.) Now all you need to do is put in the marjoram, taste. Add salt and pepper if you need it. Easy, huh? But wait...this soup is so good, you'll spend the rest of the day remembering it. Sigh. What a beautiful life!

****

What's in a sweet potato? I decided to start with the nutrition information this time. OK, here goes. You won't believe how nutritious these are! 1/2 C. cooked sweet potato contains ALL of the following: 2 g. Protein, 3.4 g Fiber, 24.6 mg. Vitamin C, 28 mg. Calcium, 22.6 mcg. Folic Acid, 20 mg. Magnesium, 348 mg. Potassium, PLUS 21,822 iu Vitamin A (beta carotene). TA-DA!!! What a veggie! Eating the skin adds even more fiber. The deeper the orange color of the sweet potato flesh, the more beta carotene.

As far as their history goes, a variety of sources have their origins as somewhere in Mexico, Central America or South America. Anyway, the American Indians of what would one day be Louisiana, were growing them in their gardens as early as 1540.

Columbus brought them back to Spain from the West Indies. The Spanish loved them and began cultivating them right away. Not long after that, Spain began exporting them to England where they were put into a spice pie and consumed voraciously at the court of Henry VIII.

The popularity of the sweet potato in France, however was fairly erratic. The

215

French would love them for a while and then get bored with them, love them again, and get bored with them...again. When the Empress Josephine came along, their popularity surged once more because she loved them. After that, they became a constant part of the French court menu.

Sweet potatoes became a staple in African and Asian diets soon after they were introduced by the Portuguese explorers. Sweet potatoes were so important in the United States, it is said they were what sustained the soldiers during the American Revolution and Civil War.

In the past 25 years, Australia and the southern, warmer areas of Russia, have developed sweet potato cultivation big time. It is however, China, who grows most of the world's sweet potato crop.

Here's one last little tidbit of information you might find interesting. A yam is NOT a sweet potato and a sweet potato is NOT a yam. A yam is tropical and not grown in the U.S., not even Hawaii. Yams are very starchy and can grow up to 100 pounds! Imagine putting one of those in your oven and topping that with marshmallows!

SOUTH OF THE BORDER LENTIL STEW
(Serves 6-8)

The flavors of this stew blend, then dance and finally burst in your mouth. It is even better after a couple days. Sometimes I prepare a double batch and invite a bunch of people over for a cozy evening. If there's any left...well, lucky me.

1-2 T. olive oil

3-4 cloves garlic, crushed

3 C. vegetable broth

1 bay leaf

1 t. salt

2 t. chili powder

1 C. carrots, sliced

1 ½ C. Chihuahua cheese grated

1 lg. onion, chopped

3 C. water

2 C. lentils, rinsed & picked over

A couple grinds of fresh pepper

2 t. cumin

1 C. celery, sliced

3 C. fresh spinach, stems removed

Optional: cooked brown rice

1.) In a 5-qt. pot, sauté onion in olive oil. Add garlic when the onion starts to turn transparent. Sauté for a few more minutes or just until the onion starts to brown around the edges. Be careful, you don't want to burn the garlic so you might want to turn the heat down a little.

2.) Next add water, vegetable broth, lentils, bay leaf, salt and pepper. Cover and simmer on low for 20 minutes.

3.) Optional: While the lentils are cooking, you can toast the cumin and chili powder. Toasting some spices enhances the flavor, making them ecstatic. Put the cumin and chili powder in a small frying pan. Over medium low heat begin to toast the spices, stirring constantly. After about three minutes, lower the heat and continue stirring for two more minutes. You will not believe how this little trick makes the flavors POP! Put the toasted spices in a small bowl until you're ready to use them. If you leave them in the pan without stirring them...they will burn, since the pan is still hot.

4.) After the lentils have simmered for 20 minutes, add the carrots, celery and toasted spices. Continue cooking over low heat without the lid, stirring occasionally. Cook until most of the liquid is absorbed and the vegetables are tender.

5.) Toss spinach in. Adjust seasonings. Heat slowly for 5 more minutes. Remove bay leaf.

6.) Spoon, piping hot, into bowls and top with cheese.

7.) If you want to make this a hardier meal or make it stretch for unexpected company, you can put a small mound of brown rice in the bowl first, top with the lentil stew and finally the cheese. I hope you're hungry.

****

Bay leaves are considered to be symbols of glory and reward. Throughout ancient Greece and Rome, scholars and poets wore wreaths of bay leaves when they achieved academic honors, which is where the term "baccalaureate" comes from. At the first Olympics in 776 B.C., bay garlands were presented to the champions.

Legend has it that the Greek god Apollo, god of healing, prophecy and poetry, was in love with a nymph named Daphne. She wanted nothing to do with him, so she changed herself into a bay tree to hide from him. A little extreme wouldn't you say? When he found out, he declared the bay tree to be sacred and wore a crown of its leaves on his head in her memory.

Romans felt the bay leaf protected them from thunder and the plague. Later on, the Italians and English thought bay brought good luck and protected them from evil spirits.

218

As for its herbal qualities, a tea made of bay has a reputation for soothing an acid stomach and relieving flatulence. It is best known however, for relieving the pain of arthritis and rheumatism. Just rub a little bay oil on the tender area and feel the heat spread. The warmth created by bay oil is also soothing for sprains, bruises and some skin rashes.

When you're using bay leaves in cooking remember a little goes a long way. One or two leaves is all it takes. The flavor is released by cooking the leaf in liquid, which means it is an excellent addition to most soups and stews. Just remember to remove the leaves before serving. You wouldn't want to get one of those caught in your throat.

GOLDEN CAULIFLOWER SOUP
(Serves 6)

An unusual mix of ingredients makes this soup stand out. It is a very calming, soothing soup...very uplifting at the end of a long day. Whenever I make this it seems that I'm put in a contemplative mood as I chop and stir. All stress melts away.

3 C. cooked spaghetti squash (good use for leftovers)*See note
2 T. olive oil
1 large onion, chopped
3-4 cloves garlic, crushed
8 C. vegetable or chicken stock
1 medium head cauliflower, cut into small flowerets
1/2 C. white wine or water
1 t. salt
A thickener made from 1 T. cornstarch and 1/2 C. water
1 C. grated carrot (thanks, Es)
2 C. cojack cheese, grated
¼ C. parmesan, grated
1 T. fresh sage, cut into slivers or 1 t. dried sage, crumbled
1/2 C. white wine or water
Salt and pepper to taste

*Note: In case you don't know how to cook spaghetti squash, relax...it's very easy. If you don't know what one is...ask your produce manager. You could substitute another squash but come on now...be adventurous. OK...using a very sharp knife, cut the stem off along with about an inch of the squash. Spaghetti squash are a hard squash so be careful! Alright...cut the squash in half, lengthwise. I tip it up on the end I just cut off and cut down through the middle. It's just easier for me. Scoop the seeds out, sprinkle lightly with salt and place them, cut side down, on a greased cookie sheet or 9 x 13 baking pan. Bake at 350 degrees for 45 minutes or until a fork easily pierces the skin. Turn the two halves face up and let them cool. Scoop out the flesh. There you have it.

1.) While the squash is baking, sauté onion in olive oil until onion is transparent. Add garlic. You might need to add a little more olive oil so the garlic doesn't stick and burn. Sauté the garlic with the onion for 2-3 minutes.

2.) Add the stock, cauliflower, wine and salt. Bring to a boil, reduce heat and simmer for about 6 minutes. Add spaghetti squash and sage. Simmer for 5 more minutes.

3.) Make thickener in small bowl. Maker sure there are no lumps. Add it and the grated carrot to the soup, stirring constantly, until soup starts to thicken.

4.) Turn off heat, stir in cheeses. Cover pot for 5 minutes until cheese melts. Add salt and pepper to taste. Adjust seasonings. Isn't this the best? It's a good way to get your kids to eat cauliflower. Serve right away.

****

Sage has quite a history! Medicinally it has been used for almost everything over the centuries. I only recently became more aware of its varied uses since working on this cookbook, even though it has been in my herb garden for years. It was voted Herb of the Year in 2001, by the International Herb Association, because of its flavor AND health-giving properties. Native to the Mediterranean Sea area, it is an excellent source of fiber and iron.

The Romans treated it as sacred and created a ceremony around gathering sage. Both the Greeks and Romans used it to preserve meat. Chinese traders swapped three cases of tea for one case of sage. Ancient Greeks used it for, hold on to your hats; kidney trouble, coughs, ulcers, rheumatism, sore throats snake bites, forgetfulness (hmmmm), grief and to get rid of gray hair. Modern Europeans use it for many of the above things PLUS gingivitis and cold sores. In my investigation of sage, I discovered the English have been using sage tea to clear eyes. I had been having trouble with burning, itchy eyes for a long time. None of the eye drops or washes I got from the health food store worked. The discouraging thing was, when my eyes got really bad, I felt tired, even though my body was raring to go. My eyes felt like they had sand in them and all I wanted to do was take a nap. Even if I did, when I woke up, my eyes still felt awful. The very day I read about sage, soothing eyes, I went into my garden, cut off a little handful of sage leaves and made the tea. Once it had cooled down, I strained a small amount into my sterilized eye cup, ahhhhh! For the first time in months my eyes did not burn. Not only that, they weren't blood shot anymore. My eyes were twinkling back at me in the mirror!

The French have been using it medicinally for centuries because it has antibacterial properties. They have been using sage tea as a preventative measure because it cleanses the inner body of germs and disease. I think fresh is better than dried. WARNING: Do not drink it if you are pregnant...it can be abortive.

MY MOST COMFORTING SOUP
(Serves 6)

The large amount of garlic and the veggies combined with the barley, make this a great soup if you think you might be "coming down with something." Of course it is wonderful anytime but I also make this when I need a big hug.

3 T. olive oil

1 C. celery, sliced

1 "head" of garlic, peel and slice cloves, yes all of it

Some white wine or water

1 C. mushrooms, sliced

1 1/2 C. frozen corn, or fresh if you've got it

12 oz. can evaporated skim milk

1 T. marjoram or 1 t. dried, if you don't have marjoram you could use basil

1 C. carrots, sliced

1 large onion, chopped

3 small zucchini, sliced

4 C. vegetable stock

¾ C. barley

3 T. flour

Parmesan to sprinkle on top

Salt and pepper to taste

1.) Sauté carrots, celery, onion and garlic, in olive oil, in a large soup pot until onion is clear. This usually takes 5-7 minutes. If the veggies start to stick, add a little white wine or water.

2.) Add zucchini, mushrooms and corn. Continue to sauté for about 5 more minutes, adding a little wine or water if it starts sticking.

3.) Stir in the vegetable broth and barley. Turn heat to low and simmer, covered, for 40 minutes or until barley is tender.

4.) Put the evaporated milk and flour in a jar. Screw the lid on the jar tightly and shake. Shake that thing! Make sure there is no flour clumped in the bottom of the jar.

5.) Bring the soup to a low boil then add flour mixture. Reduce heat and stir until soup thickens. Add the marjoram or basil and salt and pepper to taste.

6.) Serve immediately with a large sprinkle of parmesan on top. Cozy up now...doesn't that feel better? You bet it does.

****

<u>Barley</u> was the first cereal crop to be domesticated. Remains of 10,000 year old barley grains were found in the Fertile Crescent. I think I need to give you a little geography lesson concerning the Fertile Crescent, since it pops up all the time in my food history research. It is an area of fertile land in the Middle East stretching in a broad semicircle from the Nile, to the Tigris and to the Euphrates (all 3 are rivers). If you're really curious and you love learning new things, you can find it on a map of North Africa.

Ancient cultures were making barley bread long before wheat was domesticated. Because it contains so little gluten, unlike wheat, barley bread was very dense but extremely nutritious. Gluten is the protein in grain that makes bread rise easily. Wheat replaced barley in bread making because it made a lighter, more palatable loaf. However, other uses for barley were discovered. The Sumerians used it for measurement and a form of money, while the Babylonians used it for simple monetary exchange. Vedic writing mentions barley and rice as, "two immortal sons of heaven." The Babylonians created the oldest known recipe for making barley wine. The directions were discovered on a brick dating 2,800 B.C. At the same time, Emperor Shen Nun in China, named barley to be one of the five sacred cultivated plants of China.

In 1324, an English royal decree, standardized the barley inch, as being equal to 3 barleycorns laid end to end. In 1888, the U.S. shoe industry accepted this standard, which established size 13 (39 barleycorns) as the largest regularly manufactured shoe. Ahem...I think that is not the case anymore.

224

Columbus brought it to the New World in 1493 and it's been grown here ever since. Canada is one of the largest barley producers in the world. The Japanese use barley malt for a sweetener, elsewhere the grain is used for malt beer, whiskey, animal feed and even in biodegradable plastics! Today barley is the world's 4th largest crop. In the U.S. only a very small portion gets to the table...the rest is used for animal feed and to make beer.

I love barley in soup or as a replacement for rice in rice pilaf, which then is barley pilaf. One cup of barley has 31g. Fiber, 9mg. Niacin, 58 mg. Calcium, 442 mg. Phosphorus, 560mg. Potassium, 75 mcg. Selenium and has only 2.3g. Fat. Since its gluten level is so low, it is a very good grain for those who are gluten sensitive. Woo-hoo!

AU GRATIN POTATO SOUP
(Serves 4-6)

This is such a welcoming soup. Invite some friends over and make sure they bring their slippers. Maybe they'll want to pitch in and help. In no time at all, you and your chums will be gathered around the table slurping soup and swapping funny stories.

1 large onion, chopped	1 C. celery, chopped small
2-3 T. olive oil	4 C. chicken broth
4 C. potatoes, peeled and cubed	1 1/2 C. grated cheddar
2 C. milk	1/2 C. sour cream
1 t. dry thyme	Salt and freshly ground pepper to
1 head garlic	taste

1.) Sauté onion and celery in oil in a large soup pot with a lid.
2.) Meanwhile, separate and peel cloves of garlic. Cut the big cloves in half. When the onion is translucent, add broth, potatoes and garlic. Bring to a boil, reduce heat, cover and simmer until potatoes are tender.
3.) Coarsely mash potatoes, onion, celery and garlic with a potato masher. This is one you want chunks of veggies in so don't get too carried away with the mashing.
4.) Add milk, cheddar, thyme, sour cream, salt and pepper.
5.) Be careful when you heat this up. Have the heat on very low and stir frequently. Don't bring it to a boil. The soup will curdle and will look gross. The soup just needs to warm up and the cheese should barely be melted. Wasn't that easy? This is wonderful with a baby lettuce, avocado and sweet onion salad, tossed with your favorite vinaigrette. Now, all together, sing, "Heaven, I'm in Heaven..."

People might not remember what you said; people might not remember what you did; but they will ALWAYS remember how you made them feel.

A 3,000 year old Sanskrit literature mentions pepper. <u>Black pepper</u>, native to India's Malabar Coast, has been grown in Malaysia and Indonesia for at least 2,000 years. In 80 B.C., the greatest spice trading port in the Eastern Mediterranean was Alexandria, Egypt. One of its entrances was known as the "Pepper Gate."

Pepper was so precious long ago, it was used as money to pay taxes, dowries and rent. Imagine handing your landlord a bag of pepper to pay your rent nowadays! It was weighed like gold and used in almost every form of monetary exchange. In 410 A.D., when Rome was captured by Attila the Hun, 3,000 pounds of pepper were demanded as ransom. When Genovese soldiers conquered Palestine in 1101 A.D., they were each given a two pound bag of pepper as a gift.

Pepper was valued so highly, a search was initiated for a new pepper trade route which began the 15th Century, Age of Exploration. This prompted the beginning of the investigation of the New World. Not long ago, what was once the Soviet Union, had a trade agreement with India in which they would swap pepper from India, for Soviet construction equipment. Hmmmm! Pretty interesting.

Ancient Aryans used pepper to cure malaria and hemorrhoids. The Egyptians used it in their embalming process, while the Dutch and French used it to kill moths and as an insect repellant. Today, in India, it is used as an aromatic stimulant in cholera and vertigo. An infusion of whole black pepper

227

corns can be used as a gargle for sore throats and hoarseness.

Pepper is still considered the "King of Spices." The main flavor is from the essential oil, piperine. Recently I have seen pepper being used as an exotic flavor in desserts on the cooking channels. My Grandma Nicol used to sprinkle it on her cantaloupe. She said her mother always used to do it because pepper made melon taste even better. As kids, we all thought it was gross, but we never tried it. Maybe Grandma was on to something.

SMOKEY KALE SOUP WITH BOW TIES
(Serves 8)

This is an enchanting soup. There is no other way to describe it. It is so good for you but you won't even know it. The smell weaves its way throughout your house and soon everyone is wanting to know, "When's dinner?"

1 lg. sweet onion, chopped

1 15 oz. can diced tomatoes

4 C. chicken or turkey stock

1 t. allspice

1 lg. bunch kale, chopped...but don't go too far down the stems

5 cloves garlic, roughly chopped

2 C. bow tie pasta, dry

1 lb. turkey kielbasa or other precooked turkey sausage, sliced

3 T. olive oil

4 C. vegetable stock

2 T. brown sugar

1/2 C. dry white wine

1 C. carrots, sliced

1 can chickpeas

Salt and pepper to taste

1.) In a large stock pot or kettle, sauté the onion in olive oil until it starts to get transparent. Season with salt and pepper.

2.) Put in tomatoes, juice and all, both stocks, brown sugar, allspice and wine. Bring to a low boil.

3.) Add kale (make sure you have removed most of the stem), cover and reduce heat. When you first put in the kale, it will fill the pot. You'll be thinking, "Hey...isn't this way too much?" Nope. Trust me. It will cook way down...like spinach does.

4.) Simmer the kale for about 15 minutes. Slice the turkey sausage. Now check the soup. See how much the kale has cooked down? Stir it around a couple of times. Breathe in...what an aroma...and you're not done yet.

5.) Now add the turkey sausage (this will create a nice, smoky flavor to your soup), garlic, carrots, pasta and chickpeas. Stir gently, making sure every thing is well blended.

6.) Taste. Your stocks will determine how much salt and pepper you'll need. Depending on the brand or if you're using homemade, they might have enough seasoning. Well, what do you think? more salt? a couple grinds of pepper? It's up to you, sweetie.

7.) Cover and simmer for 15 minutes more until pasta is done. Serve immediately.

Store bought Onion Rosemary Foccacia is fabulous with this. The broth with the brown sugar, garlic, allspice and sausage needs nothing else. Yum!

****

To be honest, I didn't grow up with <u>kale</u>. I'd never seen it until it was on my plate as a garnish, at a restaurant. I'd also seen decorative kale in fall gardens and thought it was quite attractive but never thought you could actually eat the stuff.

Over time, I heard how nutritious it was so I did some research and discovered it REALLY is good for you. However, my mother always told me liver was good for me too (grimace). I never learned to like liver. I wondered if kale was going to be that way for me too. I had been working on a soup recipe and decided to substitute kale for the spinach. I was amazed. I loved it. I mean, I absolutely loved it! I tried the soup out on my husband...he went back for seconds. I invited some friends over and gave them some of the soup...they had seconds too! That's how "Smokey Kale Soup with Bow Ties" was born.

Kale is actually the wild ancestor of cabbage, cauliflower, broccoli and

230

Brussels sprouts. It is native to the Mediterranean area or possibly Asia Minor. Kales' botanical name, *Brassica oleracea,* variety *acephala*, translates to "cabbage of the vegetable garden without a head." It was grown as a leafy vegetable for thousands of years before it was cultivated into the other vegetables of its family.

It is thought to have been brought to Europe around 600 B.C. by Celtic wanderers. Most peasant gardens in the Middle Ages grew kale. It is cherished in the fall garden because it is extremely hardy and gets sweeter after a couple of frosts. When nothing else was growing in the garden, kale nourished people during the long, cold winter months.

It is a good source of Vitamin K, Vitamin C, Vitamin A and Folic Acid. Kale has long been honored as one of the vegetables with the highest Calcium content. In order for the human body to assimilate Calcium, Magnesium must be present. Kale has both. In addition, it also has Iron and more Protein than most vegetables.

I 'm going to grow kale in my garden next summer. There are a couple of varieties I want to try. One of my seed catalogues has a more tender variety that looks interesting. Don't you love trying new things?

Chapter 8

Breads, Muffins, Etc.

"Now are we going to 'bob' for apples?"

CRUNCHY, TOASTY BANANA MUFFINS
(Makes 12)

I love muffins. When you make them yourself with the freshest ingredients they are a true comfort food. Your house will smell glorious as these are baking. Open the doors and expect some company...or not.

2 ripe bananas, mashed   1 1/2 C. oats, toasted *
3/4 C. milk   1 1/4 C. flour
1 egg   1 T. sesame seeds, toasted*
1/3 C. honey   1 T. baking powder
1/4 C. safflower oil   1/2 t. salt
1 t. vanilla

<u>Sesame Crunch Topping</u>:
1/2 C. chopped pecans   2 T. flour, 1/2 t. cinnamon
2 T. brown sugar, packed   1/4 t. ginger
2 T. <u>sesame seeds</u>   1/4 t. cloves

Mix together then cut in 2 T. butter with a pastry blender or a fork until mixture is crumbly.

*_Note on toasting_: This is not hard. You would not believe how much toasting certain foods enhances their flavor. In a large dry frying pan, over medium heat, toast oats stirring frequently, for about 3 minutes. You will begin to get a whiff of a subtle, nutty fragrance. Keep stirring for about 2 more minutes or until they are done to your satisfaction. Let them cool slightly before adding them to the batter.

Toasting sesame seeds goes a lot quicker. In the same pan, over low heat, add the 1 T. sesame seeds, stirring constantly. They will start to pop when they

235

are almost done. Toast them until they are a beautiful golden brown. This should only take 1-2 minutes.

1.) Preheat oven to 375. Prepare muffin tin with cooking spray.
2.) In a medium-size bowl, beat the bananas, milk, egg, honey, oil and vanilla together.
3.) In a large mixing bowl, stir the flour, toasted oats, toasted sesame seeds, baking powder and salt together. Mix thoroughly.
4.) Add the banana mixture to the dry ingredients. Blend well but do not over mix. The batter will be tough if you beat it up.
5.) Fill muffin cups 2/3 full. Top with Sesame Crunch Topping and bake for 13-15 minutes.

****

<u>Sesame seeds</u> have a very ancient history. They are one of the oldest edible seeds known to man and are native to India. Archeological digs have discovered the earliest residents of the Tigris and Euphrates valley ate bread made of sesame dough. That would probably be pretty tasty, don't you think?

"Open sesame" was the magical phrase used to enter the cave in <u>Ali Baba and the Forty Thieves.</u> It refers to the fact that ripe sesame seed pods open with a sharp pop at the slightest touch.

Today the seeds are mostly used as a condiment in most of the U.S. However, in the South they are also called benne seeds and used quite frequently in all types of cooking. They are the primary source of oil in Asia and Africa and remain a staple in Middle Eastern cooking.

The seeds are high in Protein and contain about 55% oil. One cup of sesame seeds contain 99 iu. Vitamin A, 140 mcg. Folic Acid, a whopping 1404 mg. Calcium, 888 mg. Phosphorus, and 4.9 g. of the amino acid Arginine. Pretty nutritious little seed huh?

It's worth the extra time to toast the oats and sesame seeds. By the time you've cleaned up the kitchen and made a pot of tea, the muffins will be done. Quick, run outside and give a couple to a neighbor. They're such toasty, cozy muffins no one can resist. Don't bother to tell anyone, "They're good for you." No one would believe it.

We are united by the bridge of love which knows no distance. Be at peace.

HERBY CHEESE BREAD
(Makes 2 loaves)

Making bread from scratch is so satisfying. Don't get me wrong, I have a bread machine but, when I have time, I love to make homemade bread with my own two hands. This bread is so scrumptious and therapeutic to make, you'll get hooked once you've tried it. The smell, while it's baking...heaven.

2 pkgs. dry yeast

1/2 C. warm water

1 1/2 T. dehydrated chopped onion

1/3 C. honey

1/3 C. safflower oil

1 1/2 t. salt

1 C. warm water

3/4 C. milk

3 1/2 C. unbleached flour

3 T. wheat germ

2 T. ground flax seed

2 t. Herbs de Provence

1 C. amaranth flour*

1 C. whole wheat flour

2 C. cojack cheese, grated

*amaranth flour can be found at your health food store

1.) Dissolve yeast in 1/2 C. warm water, in a large mixing bowl. Add onion, honey, oil, salt, 1 C. warm water, and milk. Mix thoroughly.

2.) Stir in the unbleached flour. Beat until it's very smooth.

3.) Next add the wheat germ, flax seed, Herbs de Provence and the amaranth flour. Beat again until smooth. Are your arms getting tired? Think of the workout you're getting. You GO!!

4.) It's time to add the whole wheat flour. The dough should be fairly easy to handle now...not too sticky.

5.) On a lightly floured surface, knead dough for 5 minutes, until it is smooth and elastic. Every time the dough gets too sticky, sprinkle a little flour on it. Don't short cut this step. It's essential for the finished bread and it's good for your Soul. I know that might sound like a long time to some of you, but as you're kneading, think of all the love you have for your family, yourself, your friends, your pets...otherwise why would you be pushing a piece of dough around for so long? Homemade bread (not from a machine) is a labor of love and not as hard as many think. Like a lot of things that are worth it, it just takes time.

6.) OK, enough gabbing. After you're done kneading, place the dough in a large, greased (with a little vegetable oil) bowl; turn dough, greased side up. Cover, let rise in a warm place until it doubles. That usually takes about an hour or so. The dough is ready when you poke the dough and the indentation remains.

7.) Gently punch the dough down. This doesn't mean go crazy. My first experience with making bread was when I was a new bride a million years ago. I threw the dough around so much, I killed the yeast. One good punch is enough. Divide the dough in half. With your hands, flatten each half into a 12"x9" rectangle. Sprinkle each piece with 1 C. of the cojack cheese.

8.) Starting with one of the 9-inch sides, roll dough tightly into a big roll. Pinch ends together to seal in the cheese. Place each roll, seam side down, in a greased loaf pan.

9.) Let rise again, covered, for 1 hour. Heat oven to 375 degrees, 350, if you're using glass pans. Place pans in the center of the oven and bake for 35-45 minutes. When they're done, the bread will be a deep golden brown and sound hollow when you tap them.

10.) Remove the pans from the oven. Keep the bread in the pans for 10 minutes, then run a knife around the edges of each pan. Remove the loaves and let them cool on a wire rack at least 30 minutes before you slice into a loaf.

11.) You'll probably want to have a piece while it's still warm. Make sure you use a serrated knife and cut in a light sawing motion...otherwise your beautiful loaves of bread will squish down to an inch tall. Now...butter...no butter. It's up to you.

MMMMM! Wasn't it worth it?

****

OK, the highlight of this recipe is a very underused ingredient...<u>wheat germ</u>. It's packed with nutrition and has a great nutty flavor when it's toasted.

Wheat germ is at the heart of every wheat kernel but only makes up about 2½% of the whole kernel. (Just an aside here. Did you know it takes approximately 1 million kernels of wheat to fill a bushel basket?) It is loaded with Vitamin E, Folic Acid, Phosphorus, Thiamin, Zinc and Magnesium. Also it has more B-complex than any other food except liver. One tablespoon of wheat germ contains 1g. of fiber. Pretty impressive.

An easy way to add this nutritious little bugger to your baking is to replace 1/4 C. of flour with wheat germ. You can do this for every 2 C. flour. I've done this with chocolate chip cookies. It adds a nice nutty flavor and my kids never knew. You can also freeze it without losing its nutritional value.

STRAWBERRY CREAM MUFFINS
(Makes 12)

These are so simple to make. Dried fruits, your choice, have a very intense flavor which are perfect for baking. Whip up a batch of these on a lazy Saturday morning and see how fast everyone comes charging into the kitchen.

2 C. unbleached flour

1 T. baking powder

1/2 t. salt

1/8 t. freshly ground nutmeg

1 t. lemon peel

1/3 C. plus 1 T. honey

1/2 t. lemon extract

2 eggs, slightly beaten

2/3 C. buttermilk

1/4 C. butter, melted

1/2 C. dried strawberries, cherries, blueberries or cranberries

Topping: 1/4 c. chopped pecans and 2 T. brown sugar. Mix together and set aside.

1.) Prepare a muffin tin by either spraying it with cooking spray or buttering the individual muffin cups and then dusting them with flour. Oh heck, use the spray...it's much quicker.

2.) Sift the flour, baking powder, salt, and nutmeg together. Stir in the lemon peel.

3.) Into the dry ingredients, add the honey, lemon extract, eggs, buttermilk and melted butter. Blend thoroughly.

4.) Fold in the dried fruit. If you want to get really daring, you can use more than one kind of fruit.

5.) Fill each muffin cup about 2/3 full. Sprinkle on topping. Bake at 350 degrees for 18-20 minutes. Cool for about 5 minutes before removing them from the pan.

Now sit back and relax with a freshly baked muffin and a cup of your favorite tea or coffee. Ahhh! Does it really ever get any better than that? Nope!

IT IS NOT IN DOING WHAT YOU LIKE, BUT IN LIKING WHAT YOU DO THAT IS THE SECRET OF HAPPINESS.

-James M. Barrie

Here is a fact that might surprise you about <u>buttermilk</u>: there is no butter in it! Also, it is lower in fat than regular milk. Most of the buttermilk we get today is cultured. Originally, homemade buttermilk was the slightly sour, residual liquid that remains after butter is churned. So you see, it was actually, "milk of the butter." It also had tiny flecks of butter in it. Its flavor is much like that of plain yogurt. It takes one gallon of milk to make a half pint of real buttermilk. Most people like it very cold. My Grandma Nicol used to drink cold buttermilk mixed with tomato juice. It looked pretty in the glass, but the thought of it still makes me grimace. Well, actually, I shouldn't make a face unless I've tried it. That's what I always say to my kids anyway.

Like I mentioned before, most buttermilk today is labeled cultured buttermilk. This means a lactic acid is added to sweet pasteurized milk. This milk is then left to ferment for 12-14 hours at about 69 degrees. It is a lot thicker than original buttermilk. Most people I talked to use it only when they make ranch salad dressing from the packet. I have it on hand all the time for baking (plus making ranch dressing). I discovered over the years, that you can reduce the fat, by half, in your muffin, bread and scone recipes, by substituting buttermilk. Say, for example, your recipe calls for 1/2 C. butter. You can use 1/4 C. butter and 1/4 C. buttermilk, and not lose any of the flavor. Another plus, the buttermilk also keeps whatever you're baking moist...unlike when you use applesauce as a fat substitute. I've had some very dry muffins trying that trick.

Irish folklore says a glass of buttermilk will cure a hangover and when heated with a clove of garlic, will cure a lot of other ailments. American folklore declared drinking buttermilk would immunize you against poison oak and poison ivy. That's not one I'm willing to experiment with. If you don't have any buttermilk around, you can make a substitute by adding 1 T. of lemon juice to 1 C. of milk and let it stand for 10 minutes.

One cup of buttermilk has only 99 Calories and is a good source of Folic Acid, Calcium, Phosphorus, Potassium and Selenium. It also has only 1.34g Saturated Fat compared to 2.92 Saturated Fat for an equal amount of 2% milk. On top of that, buttermilk has only 9mg of Cholesterol! It's a pretty healthy item to have on hand, as you can see, by how moist and yummy these Strawberry Cream Muffins are.

CEREBRAL PANCAKES
(Makes 12-14 pancakes)

This was the first recipe, created by me, that I ever wrote down. I have been cooking since I was 12 and some of my creations are better left forgotten. Over the years though, I'd developed into quite a culinary architect. As we were eating these pancakes, I read the information on the amaranth flour package. FLASH! This was interesting. Flour that was good for memory. I suddenly got the urge to record the recipe and how amaranth would benefit the body. I grabbed my trusty yellow legal pad and the rest is history. When you try these, you'll be tickling your taste buds as well as renewing your brain cells.

3/4 C. unbleached flour	1 T. Oil
1/2 C. amaranth flour	1 C. skim milk
2 T. sugar	1/3 C. buttermilk
2 t. non-aluminum baking powder	1 egg
1/2 t. salt	3/4 C. chunky applesauce
1 t. cinnamon	1/2 C. chopped pecans, toasted
Safflower oil	

1.) Mix both flours, sugar, baking powder, salt and cinnamon together in a medium-sized bowl.
2.) In a separate bowl, whisk oil, skim milk, buttermilk and egg together. Add to dry ingredients. Stir until just blended.
3.) Gently fold in applesauce and nuts. Now you're ready to go.
4.) Heat a large skillet. Baste skillet lightly with safflower oil. Pour scant 1/4 cup of batter onto skillet for each pancake.
5.) CREATIVE OPTION: You could make a couple big ones or if you really want to wake up the troops, make them into shapes. Whatever pops your cork.

6.) Cook until bubbly and the edges appear dry. Flip (the pancake, not you). Place on warm platter and keep warm.

7.) Repeat until all the batter is gone. Serve with butter, warmed syrup, apple butter or honey. Yummy!

****

In Mexico, the <u>amaranth</u> plant was domesticated at about 5,000 B.C. It was a staple in ancient Aztec, Incan and Mayan diets. Once believed to have supernatural powers, it was incorporated into Aztec religious ceremonies. Before the Spanish conquest, amaranth flour was used in conjunction with human sacrifice. The Spanish conquerors were so appalled by this, they decided if they eliminated amaranth, the sacrifices would be eradicated. Growing amaranth was forbidden. Amaranth almost became extinct for hundreds of years. A few isolated pockets of it were grown in the Andes and southern Mexico...that is why we still know of it today.

In Mexico and Peru, young amaranth leaves, which taste a lot like spinach, are gathered and eaten as a vegetable. Some countries pop the seeds (like popcorn), mix it with sugar or honey, and eat it as a treat. Boiling water can be poured over the flowers to make an infusion, which can then be drunk to "cleanse the blood," after adding a little rum, of course.

Amaranth, translated from Greek, means "never-fading flower." It is an annual herb that really isn't a true grain. There are approximately 60 species with no particular distinction made between the varieties grown for its leaves and the varieties grown for seed (flour).

OK, enough of the technical stuff. You can get amaranth flour at your health food store and sometimes even the larger grocery stores...if you ask nicely.

Since amaranth has no gluten, you need to add wheat flour if you are baking something that needs to rise. Otherwise, feel free to use it as often as you can. It has a...oh, I don't know...um...smooth, nutty flavor.

BUT, the main reason you want to use it as often as possible, is because it is a nutrition powerhouse!!! First of all, it is loaded with Lysine and Methionine which are essential amino acids. Now these particular amino acids are excellent for brain function, particularly memory and thinking skills. One fourth cup of amaranth flour has 3 times the Fiber and 5 times the Iron, than that of wheat flour. It also has 2 times more Calcium than milk, no Cholesterol PLUS 15-18% Protein in that little quarter cup. Got a big test coming up? a big presentation? Hurry to the kitchen and make a batch of Cerebral Pancakes. You'll be ready for anything.

ORANGE PECAN SCONES
(Makes 12)

If you've never made scones before, but you have had them at a tea or a coffee shop...well...how proud of yourself do you think you will be when you whip up a batch of these?

1 egg	3/4 C. buttermilk
2 T. honey	2 t. orange rind
Juice from one orange	3 1/4 C. flour
2 T. wheat germ	2 t. baking powder
1 t. baking soda	1/2 t. salt
1/2 t. cinnamon	½ C. cold butter, cubed
1/2 C. toasted, chopped pecans	Sprinkle of brown sugar

1.) Preheat oven to 375 degrees. In a medium-sized bowl, whisk together the egg, buttermilk, honey, orange rind and orange juice.

2.) In a large bowl, sift together, the flour, wheat germ, baking powder, baking soda, salt and cinnamon. Make sure the dry ingredients are well mixed.

3.) Cut the butter up in small chunks and toss them into the dry ingredients. Using a pastry blender, a large fork or your hands, cut the butter into the flour mixture until it becomes coarse crumbs...a little like lumpy cornmeal.

4.) Now add the wet ingredients to the dry ingredients. Stir only until just blended. After this point you DO NOT want to OVERWORK the dough. Gently stir in the pecans.

5.) Turn the dough out onto lightly floured surface. It might be a little sticky but that's ok...just sprinkle a tablespoon of flour onto the top and knead 2 or 3 times. Too much kneading makes your scones tougher. We want tender and flaky OK?

6.) With your hands, shape the dough into a circle about 12 inches across. It is up to you how you want to shape your scones. You can cut the dough into 12 equal pie-shaped pieces or make round scones using a biscuit cutter or a glass (about 3 inches across) dipped in flour.

7.) Put the scones on a baking sheet lined with parchment paper or sprayed with cooking spray. Sprinkle each with a little brown sugar. Bake at 375 for 12-15 minutes. Serve warm with butter, jam and honey. How long has it been since you felt this snuggly?

****

Honey is truly one of God's gifts to humanity. It is the oldest known sweet to human kind. Honey is the only natural food that is made without destroying any kind of life. What about that?!! Early references to honey have been discovered as far back as 4,000 B.C., where Egyptians used honey as a tribute or in payment for a debt. In the Bible, Israel and Palestine were referred to as "the land of milk and honey." Ancient Greeks offered it to their gods and spirits of the dead. Mead, an alcoholic drink made with honey, was considered to be the drink of the gods.

In 1683, European settlers introduced honey bees to New England. In addition to food preparation, it was used to make cement (?), furniture polish, varnish, to preserve fruit and for medicinal purposes. Abe Lincoln loved his bread smeared with honey and "bee bread" (honeycomb containing pollen and honey).

In Babylon, 4000 years ago, after a wedding, the bride's father traditionally supplied the groom with all the mead or honey beer the groomed wanted for the first month of marriage. At that time, the calendar was moon based. Do you see where this is going? This period was called the "honey month" or what we call it today...the honeymoon.

A wonderful way to pamper yourself...female or male, is to give yourself a honey facial. Wrap your hair up in a towel. Wash your face and then apply a thin coat of honey to your face. Lie down with your feet up and listen to some fabulous music. Don't put too much honey on because the heat of your body causes the honey to become runny. A little runny is OK a lot of runny is a big mess. After 15-20 minutes, rinse your face with warm water, pat dry and apply your favorite moisturizer. I promise, your face will feel as soft as when you were a child. The honey sucks dirt and toxins right out of your skin. Ahhh!

I want to tell you about an undiscovered treasure between Milwaukee and Madison, Wisconsin. In 1852, German immigrant C.F. Diehnelt started Honey Acres with his beekeeping talents. Their 40 acre property, in Ashippun, Wisconsin, has a professionally designed "Honey of a Museum" and a shop where they sell all kinds of honey, honey creme, honey mustard and a lot of other honey-related items. If you're ever near there or on a road trip, stop by. Here's their information:

Honey Acres
N1557 Hwy 67
Ashippun, Wisconsin 53003
Phone: 1-800-558-7745
www.honeyacres.com.

EXTRA MOIST PUMPKIN MUFFINS
(Makes 12)

These fragrant muffins are not too sweet, but are very moist and pack a lot of fiber. You'll love them on a cool day. Make cinnamon tea, put your feet up and bite into this pillow of a muffin. Oh yes...isn't life just too grand for words?

1 C. twig-type bran cereal	1/2 C. milk
1 C. cooked pumpkin	1/2 C. safflower oil
1 egg, slightly beaten	2/3 C. honey
1 1/3 C. flour	1 t. baking soda
1 T. baking powder	1 t. cinnamon
½ t, ginger	½ t. ground cloves
¼ t. freshly ground nutmeg	1/3 C. dried, sweetened
½ t. salt	cranberries
1/3 C. chopped pecans	

Topping:

3 T. brown sugar, packed	2 T. finely chopped pecans
1 T. wheat germ	1 t. cinnamon

1.) Preheat oven to 375 degrees. Prepare your muffin tin by spraying it with cooking spray. Soak the cereal in the milk, in a small bowl for about 10 minutes, while you begin preparing the rest of the batter.

2.) In a good-sized mixing bowl blend the pumpkin, oil, egg and honey. Whisk well making sure there are no big lumps.

3.) In a separate bowl, sift together the flour, baking soda, baking powder, cinnamon, ginger, cloves, nutmeg and salt.

4.) Add the milk-soaked cereal to the pumpkin and egg mixture. Blend well.

5.) Bit by bit add the sifted, dry ingredients to the wet ingredients. Make sure everything is mixed completely.

6.) Stir in the cranberries and pecans. Fill the muffin cups about 2/3 full.

7.) Prepare topping by mixing the brown sugar, pecans, wheat germ and cinnamon. Sprinkle over each muffin.

8.) Bake at 375 degrees for 15-20 minutes. It all depends on your oven. The muffins are done if a toothpick comes out clean when inserted in the middle of one of the muffins. Aren't you in love with the smell in your kitchen? If anyone's home they're going to rush in to see what you've been up to. Good job! I knew you could do it!

****

A couple of my sources said the oldest <u>pecans</u>, from an archaeological dig, were found along the Mississippi River in Iowa dating all the way back to 5330 B.C. Fossil evidence indicates they originated in central Texas and northern Mexico. In fact, they are the only major nut tree that grows naturally in North America.

The word pecan comes from the Indian word, "pacane," which means "tall nuts requiring a stone to crack." Because wild pecans were widely available, many tribes from North America and Mexico used them as a major food source. They were such an important food source during the fall and winter, that many migratory Indian tribes planned their movements around the fall pecan harvest. Native Indians were the first to cultivate pecan trees.

Another of the first known cultivars were the Spanish colonists and the Franciscans in northern Mexico who began pecan tree cultivation in the late 1600's to early 1700's. The first U.S. plantings took place on Long Island, New York in 1772. By the late 1700's, pecan trees were appearing in the gardens of George Washington and Thomas Jefferson.

An African American slave from Louisiana, Antoine, who was considered a brilliant gardener, successfully propagated a magnificent variety of pecan tree by grafting a top-quality wild pecan with a seedling pecan. Antoine's clone was named "Centennial" because it won Best Pecan Exhibited Award in the Philadelphia Centennial Exposition of 1876. These trees flourished so well, they eventually increased to 126 Centennial trees. They were the first official planting of improved pecan trees in the United States. Way to go Antoine!

I bet you don't know how utterly nutritious pecans are. Each ounce has about 190 Calories, 2g of Protein and no Cholesterol. The fat they contain is mostly unsaturated. The American Dietetic Association says they can actually lower bad Cholesterol (LDL). They are also a good source of Fiber, Potassium, Thiamine, Zinc, Copper, Magnesium, Phosphorus, Niacin, Folic Acid, Iron and Vitamin B6. How about that? Pecans make an excellent snack food. Grab a handful. Yummy!

GRANDMA SCHULZE'S BANANA BREAD
(Makes 1 loaf)

Grandma Schulze lived next door when I was growing up. She wasn't actually blood related but my brothers and I loved her. She baked the most wonderful banana bread. She gave the recipe to my Mom and eventually...I got it! I tweaked it just a bit and this is what I came up with. It is a very simple recipe but it's not like most banana breads...it is VERY moist...almost pudding-like in the center. Yuuuummmmy!!!

3 ripe <u>bananas</u>, mashed	1 C. organic brown sugar*
½ C. butter, melted	2 eggs
2 t. vanilla	2 C. flour
1 t. salt	1 t. baking soda
3 T. ground flax seed	1 t. cinnamon

*The last time I made this recipe, instead of the brown sugar, I used xylitol, a natural sugar substitute. Xylitol is actually OK for diabetics (if you're diabetic, check it out) plus it helps your teeth and gums stay strong. It also fights gingivitis. Go to Dr. David Williams' website, www.drdavidwilliams.com. He's been studying it for years. I highly respect his opinion. Xylitol is a natural substance, made from corn and doesn't have a high glycemic index number. This is the first recipe I ever tried it on. I honestly could not tell the difference. You can get it at your health food store.

Caution: Xylitol is not safe for pets.

1.) Preheat your oven to 325 degrees.
2.) Mix the bananas, brown sugar, butter, eggs and vanilla together.
3.) In a larger bowl, sift the flour, salt and baking soda together. Stir in

the flax seed and cinnamon.

4.) Now pour the banana mixture into the flour mixture. Blend until well mixed.

5.) Spray the sides and bottom of a loaf pan with cooking spray. Pour the batter in. Bake for 65-75 minutes or until a toothpick inserted in the center comes out clean.

6.) Let cool, in the pan, on a wire rack for 10 minutes. Run a knife around the edges and remove loaf from pan. Let cool for at least 20 minutes before you cut it. I know it's hard. Try a slice plain, with a dab of butter or a slather of cream cheese.

My brothers and I used to wait for the middle pieces. That's the part that's like banana pudding-custard. OOOOOH!

****

There is so much nutritional and healing information about <u>bananas</u>, it's mind-boggling. The first bananas were being cultivated over 6,000 years ago in the Indus Valley (what is today Pakistan and western India), according to archeological sites in that area. Malaysia though, is considered to be the true origin of the banana for most food historians. There is also a debate on whether the apple or the banana is the world's most popular fruit. To me it really doesn't matter. They each have their own unique merits.

Bananas have been mentioned in ancient Buddhist writings and it is thought that Alexander the Great tasted his first banana in 327 B.C. while on his campaign. Many sources credit him for bringing the banana out of India and introducing it to the Mediterranean area. An interesting little tidbit about the banana tree is that it is not really a tree at all, it is the world's largest HERB!!!! Bet you didn't know that. I didn't.

254

Bananas are loaded with Potassium...602mg in a nine inch banana to be exact. That same banana has only 140 Calories, 2g of Protein, 4g of Fiber and only 2mg of Sodium. It has so many vitamins and minerals it's no wonder many nutritionists call it the perfect food.

Read on to see what I found about bananas, based on the latest research. Because they have a relatively high Iron content, bananas may help people with anemia. They can help lower blood pressure because of their high Potassium/low Sodium content. Research has shown Potassium-packed fruit may assist children in learning, by making them more alert. Make sure your kids start off the day with a banana or put one in their lunch. Mild depression may also be helped by bananas because they contain Tryptophan which makes you feel more relaxed and helps you to get a grip on mood swings. Bananas have a natural antacid effect on the digestive system because they neutralize acid and reduce irritation of the stomach lining.

The inside of the banana peel takes the itch and swelling out of mosquito bites. You can also bandage a piece (inside of peel) over a wart and ZAP! gone. I tried this on a wart that kept coming back for years. It took two weeks but it worked.

One last thing I discovered, The New England Journal of Medicine reports that you may be able to reduce your risk of stroke by 40% if you eat bananas regularly!!!! Gads, how multitalented can you get? Don't you want to run out and get a bunch?

Chapter 9

Desserts, Sort of

"I want the first piece."
"No, I want the first piece."

FRUITS OF EDEN SAUCE
(Makes about 3 cups)

This is a wonderful topping on ice cream, instead of hot fudge. You could put it on your oatmeal or smear it on toast spread with cream cheese. What about spooning it on vanilla pudding? It's quick to make and smells fabulous while it's cooking. The combination of these fruits and spices will drive you *wild*.

2 Bartlett or Anjou <u>pears</u>, chopped
1 medium Fuji apple, chopped
2 medium peaches, chopped
2 T. butter
2-3 T. brown sugar

1 t. cinnamon
1/2 t. allspice
2 T. water
1/3 C. chopped nuts, you pick

1.) Over medium low heat, sauté chopped fruit in butter for about 5 minutes. If it starts to dry out (that will depend on how juicy your fruit is), add a little water. Sometimes the juice of the fruit is enough.

2.) Add the brown sugar, cinnamon, allspice, 2 T. water and chopped nuts. Cook over medium heat until liquid starts to thicken, stirring occasionally. It will start to form a caramel-like syrup.

3.) It's done. Doesn't it smell marvelous? Put this over very cold vanilla ice cream and well...anything could happen.

AS MY DAD WOULD SAY:
I SCREAM, YOU SCREAM,
WE ALL SCREAM FOR
ICE CREAM!

Pears are another fruit that originated in China or western Asia. The pear has been cultivated since at least 2,000 B.C. Since then, about 5,000 varieties have been developed! Amazing! In a book I found on flower essences, the citizens of the legendary continent of Atlantis used the "essence of pear" to increase the creative inspiration of their musicians. Hmm!

Pear production is second only to apples worldwide. The flavor of the pear is sometimes compared to wine. Speaking of wine...have you ever had pear wine? Divine. Anyway, the Bartlett pear has been described as a "rich muscatel."

The grittiness of some pears is characteristic of oriental species, many of which have been crossed with European species to improve their resistance to disease. Because of this, some oriental varieties are called sand pears. If they are picked before they are fully ripe, the grittiness is lessened. The unripe pear continues to ripen after it is picked. If they are hard when you buy them at the grocery store, put them in a paper bag and set them on your counter for several days. That should do the trick.

Did you ever see Meg Ryan and Nicholas Cage do their pear scene in, "A City of Angels?" If you love pears and are a complete romantic, rent the movie just to see them describe eating pears to each other. Whew! It makes you want to run out, buy some great pears, and eat them with someone you love.

Up until five or six years ago, the only pears I would eat were Bartlett pears. I saw other pears at the grocery store but I passed them by. One day one of my best friends, Mary Anne, handed me a perfectly ripe Anjou pear. I was stunned. I had one when I was a child but it was as hard as a rock and tasted like one. ICK! This one was soft, slightly grainy, sweet and fragrant. It seemed to melt in my mouth. Since then, I have tried and loved, Red Bartlett and Bosc pears too.

Nutritionally, pears are pretty good for you. They have lots of Folic Acid and Potassium. They contain no Sodium or Cholesterol and have only 98 Calories in a medium-sized pear. Not to mention...they taste...hmmm. How do YOU think they taste?

GRANDMA NICOL'S STRAWBERRY SHORTCAKE
(Serves 5)

The first time I visited my grandparents in Oregon, I fell in love with the state. I wasn't in their house for more than five minutes when my grandfather took me into their kitchen and told me to close my eyes. My grandmother popped a huge strawberry into my mouth. It was so juicy and sweet. I will never forget that flavor. This is her basic recipe with a little tweaking (I can't help myself) from me. I think she'd approve.

2 lb. fresh, sliced <u>strawberries</u>

1-2 T. organic cane sugar

¼ C. whole wheat pastry flour

1 ½ C. unbleached flour

scant t. salt

1 T. baking powder

1 t. ground ginger

¼ C. organic cane sugar

¼ C. vegetable shortening

¼ C. cold butter, cut up

1 egg slightly beaten

1/3 C. cold milk

grated lemon peel from one lemon

1 C. whipping cream

1-2 T. maple syrup or brown sugar

1.) Take ½ C. of your sliced berries and smush them with a potato masher. Mix them back into the rest of the strawberries. Add 1-2 T. cane sugar, adjusting to how sweet your berries are. The smushing and the sugar make more juice to soak into the shortcake. Yum! Put them in the fridge.

2.) Turn your oven on to 450 degrees. Sift both flours, the salt, baking powder and ginger together in a large bowl. Stir in the sugar. Add the shortening and pieces of cold butter. Cut the butter and shortening into the dry ingredients using a pastry blender or a fork. Blend until it looks like coarse meal. This step makes your shortcake a little crisp on the outside and very tender on the inside.

262

3.) Stir in the egg, milk and lemon peel. Mix until the dry ingredients are just incorporated. The dough will be very stiff. That's OK, it's supposed to be.

4.) Turn the dough out onto a lightly floured surface. Knead a couple times to make the dough smoother. Now shape it into a big circle about 1 inch thick.

5.) Using a biscuit cutter or a juice glass that is approximately three inches across, cut out the shortcakes. You will have to reshape the dough a couple times to get five shortcakes.

6.) Place them on a lightly sprayed cookie sheet. Bake at 450 degrees for 10-12 minutes or until they are a light golden color.

7.) While the shortcakes are cooling, whip your cream. Like a lot of the other recipes in this book, you have a choice to make. To sweeten the whipped cream do you want to use brown sugar or maple syrup? Two tablespoons of maple syrup does give a definite maple-y taste. If you like maple syrup, this could be the way to go. If you're not sure, use the brown sugar. Make sure the bowl and cream are nice and cold. Beat until you get fairly stiff peaks. Don't whip the cream too far in advance or it will separate. Also, make sure your shortcakes are completely cooled before you assemble this. Otherwise the whipped cream will break down and you will have a mess. It will still taste all right but it won't be pretty.

8.) Now to assemble. Cut the cooled shortcake in half, cross-wise. Put a couple spoonfuls of the strawberries, with some juice, on the bottom half. Put a glob of whipped cream on top of that. Place the second half on top of the whipped cream. You're doing fine, you're almost done. Top the second half with more strawberries. Finally a little more whipped cream. If you want to, you can put a sliced berry on the very top. Doesn't that look great? Taste it. Isn't that the best shortcake ever?

The strawberry's history goes back over 2,200 years. They grew wild in Italy as far back as 234 B.C. They were discovered in Virginia by Europeans when their ships first landed. American Indians have been cultivating them since 1643. In fact, American Indians were the first to make a form of the strawberry shortcake we know today. They used to mix mashed strawberries with cornmeal and bake them.

Dr. William Butler, a 17th century writer, said, in reference to the strawberry, "Doubtless God could have made a better berry, but doubtless God never did." One of the legends I discovered was, if you break a double strawberry in half and share it with someone, they will fall in love with you. Anyone want to try and see if this works? Let me know. Madame Talien, a member of Napoleon's court, was famous for bathing in the juice of strawberries. Each bath required 22 pounds of strawberries. Fortunately or maybe unfortunately, bathing at that time, was fairly infrequent.

Strawberries have no Fat or Cholesterol and are rich in Vitamin C & B, Potassium, Folic Acid and Fiber. Thanks Gram!

RAINBOW PARFAIT
(Serves 4)

This will send you to Heaven on a hot summer day. Chill the whole fruit ahead of time. I promise, you'll be on Cloud Nine if you do. Also put a medium-sized bowl in the fridge now, so when you whip the cream in a little while, the bowl will be just right for whipping cream.

2 C. strawberries, sliced

2 mangos, peeled and cut into chunks

2 nectarines or peaches, sliced and cut into chunks

2-3 kiwi peeled and sliced

1 C. green grapes

1 ½ C. blueberries

2 Friar plums (the deep purpley-red ones), cut into chunks

2 T. fresh lemon juice to keep the fruit perky

1-2 T. brown sugar

Parfait Cream (recipe follows)

Parfait Cream:

1 8 oz. pkg. low fat cream cheese, at room temperature

½ C. whipping cream

¼ C. honey

1 t. vanilla

1.) Put all the prepared fruit into a large bowl. Toss the fruit with the lemon juice. Add the brown sugar. How much brown sugar you use depends on the sweetness of the fruit. Put the fruit in the fridge to keep it chilly.

2.) Now for the parfait cream...beat the cream cheese until fluffy. Remember that bowl you put in the fridge to whip the cream? Pull it out.

Pour the cream, honey and vanilla in. Whip until the cream has fairly stiff peaks.

3.) Now fold your fluffy cream cheese and whipped cream together. Be gentle. We're going for light and billowy here. Just like a cloud. That's perfect!

4.) To serve you can use any kind of stemmed glass you like. A water, champagne, martini or wine glass...whatever suits your fancy. Alternate layers of the fruit and cream, beginning with the fruit. You have a lot more fruit than parfait cream so you'll have to ration the cream a little. If you want more parfait cream just double the recipe. Doesn't that look elegant? Better yet...it tastes perfectly divine.

****

One of my absolute favorite foods on the entire planet is a perfectly ripe mango. If you've never had one you honestly don't know what you're missing. Every once in a while I come across champagne mangos. They are smaller with a more golden color than the ones we usually see.

Anyway...mangos originated in India and Southeast Asia over 5,000 years ago. In India, they hold a revered status. As legend would have it, Buddha was given a mango grove as a gift so he could relax underneath the towering trees. (A mango tree can grow to 60 feet tall!) Today, giving a gift of mangos is considered a gift of love or friendship in some cultures.

A Hindu legend tells a story of a mango tree growing out of the ashes of a princess, who had been incinerated by an evil sorceress. The emperor fell in love with the mango flower and its fruit. When the mango ripened and fell to the ground, the beautiful sun princess emerged. Of course they lived happily ever after.

The mango is the most widely consumed fruit in the world. It is extensively cultivated in many tropical climates, including southern Florida and Hawaii. In various parts of the world it is known as the "King Fruit." Sometimes it is picked green and eaten like a vegetable with salt and pepper. I personally have never tried it that way, but what the heck, maybe I will some day.

Mangos are jam-packed with nutrients that are soooo good for the body. When a mango is green, the amount of Vitamin C is higher, but as the fruit ripens the amount of Vitamin A (Beta Carotene) increases. Mangos also contain an enzyme that is soothing to the stomach. An average mango can contain up to 40% of your daily Fiber requirement. 3 ½ oz of mango contain 3,890 iu Vitamin A, 156 mg Potassium and 27 mg of Vitamin C.

GOOEY CHOCOLATE DESSERT SCONES
(Makes 12)

I have experimented with this recipe for quite a while to get it exactly right. I was looking for a slightly crisp outside, yet I also wanted a soft, tender inside with plenty of warm, melted chocolate in each bite. I finally got it. You can have these plain with a cup of tea or coffee or you can dress them up with fresh whipped cream and your favorite berries.

1 C. buttermilk

1/3 C. honey

½ C. unsweetened cocoa powder

¾ t. baking soda

10 T. cold butter

1 egg, slightly beaten

2 ½ C. unbleached flour

2 t. baking powder

½ t. salt

3.5 oz. 70% dark chocolate

Glaze:

1 1/2 C. powdered sugar, sifted

2 t. corn syrup

1 t. vanilla

1-2 T. milk

Optional:

Whipped cream

Fresh berries...your choice

1.) In a small bowl, mix together buttermilk, egg and honey. Blend well to make sure the honey is incorporated.

2.) In a large bowl, sift the flour, cocoa powder, baking powder, baking soda and salt together. Cut in the cold butter with a pastry blender or fork.

3.) Now add the buttermilk mixture. Stir until just mixed.

4.) Rough chop the chocolate and add to dough. Don't over mix. Too much mixing and the scones won't be tender.

5.) Instead of turning the dough onto a lightly floured surface, I used some more of the unsweetened cocoa powder. Knead a few times...not much...to make the dough smooth.

6.) Flatten the dough in to a circle about an inch thick. Cut the circle into quarters, then each quarter into three. See? Now you have twelve.

7.) Place the wedges of dough on a greased cookie sheet and bake at 375 degrees for 12-15 minutes. I find if I bake them more toward the 15 minutes, they are not as tender, but that's my oven.

8.) While they are baking, make the glaze. When they are just out of the oven, drizzle glaze over each scone. Don't they smell fantastic? I love them warm all by themselves but when my raspberry bushes are loaded, I make a batch of these scones and smother them with whipped cream and fresh picked raspberries. It honestly doesn't get much better than that.

****

There is some evidence that the Olmec Indians of the eastern Mexico lowlands, were the first to grow cocoa beans, around 1300 B.C. to 400 B.C. Cocoa beans come from cacao trees, which are grown all over the world today. As early as 500 A.D. the Mayans were writing about cacao on their pottery.

Columbus was the first European to come in contact with cocoa beans, which were used as currency by some of the native people of the New World. He brought cocoa beans back to Spain to King Ferdinand and Queen Isabella. I don't think the royal ones were very impressed at first. Later, the Spanish explorer Cortez, realized the commercial potential of the little cocoa beans. While he was busy conquering Mexico, he saw the Aztec Indians preparing a royal <u>chocolate</u> drink known as xocalatl. This was a bitter drink often flavored with chili powder. In 1519, it was reported that Emperor Montezuma drank more than 50 cups a day and served it frequently in golden goblets to his Spanish guests. Most of his Spanish visitors didn't care for it unless it was sweetened with cane sugar. Cortez brought back three chests of cocoa beans for his king and queen. Once back in Spain the hot drink was also flavored with honey, vanilla and cinnamon.

Spanish monks began processing the cocoa beans. For a long time Spain kept chocolate a closely guarded secret. Eventually, chocolate drinking spread to France then England. In 1657, the first of many English Chocolate Houses appeared for the wealthy to come and spend an afternoon sipping hot chocolate. Mass production of chocolate enabled the price to drop from $3.00 a pound to a rate that was more affordable for more people. In the middle 1800's solid eating chocolate was introduced and in 1876, in Switzerland, Daniel Peter thought of a way to add milk, thereby - milk chocolate.

Chocolate contains flavanoids, antioxidants that protect the body from free radicals. These are the same antioxidants in red wine, green tea and berries. Choose the bittersweet kind of chocolate. It has less sugar. A typical chocolate bar has the same amount of antioxidants as a 5 oz. glass of red wine.

IF YOU LOVE SOMEONE, NEVER STOP TELLING
THEM HOW WONDERFUL AND BEAUTIFUL THEY ARE

SPECIAL APPLE PUDDING
(Serves 6)

"What makes this apple pudding so special?" you might ask. It's not an old family favorite. It's the last recipe I created for a cookbook I have loved doing. One crisp, fall afternoon I was taking a walk near my home. I walked by an old Civil War cemetery where eight or ten gigantic sugar maples are planted. Their golden color against the brilliant blue sky took my breath away. I wandered around the cemetery with its ancient headstones and sat on a bench enjoying the glorious day and the peace and quiet.

I needed one more recipe for the dessert section of, Cooking with Spirit. One of the things I love about fall is the huge variety of apples that are available. I had just bought a half bushel of Mutsu apples and was wondering what I could do with them other than make apple sauce or apple pie. All of a sudden this recipe popped into my head. There is no milk or cream in it so I guess is doesn't really qualify as a true pudding but you know the texture pudding has as it rolls around on your tongue? This has it...and the flavor, well what can I say? If this doesn't give you warm fuzzies I don't know what will.

6 C. unpeeled baking apples, like Granny Smith or Mutsu, cut into small chunks

2 T. lemon juice

¼ C. water

1/3 C. sugar

1 ½ t. cinnamon, divided

½ t. ginger

¾ C. flour

3 T. brown sugar, not packed

½ t. salt

6 T. cold butter, cubed

½ C. pecans, chopped

1.) Preheat oven to 375 degrees. In a medium bowl toss apples with lemon juice and water. Put in a 9x9 buttered baking dish.

271

2.) Mix the 1/3 C. sugar with 1 t. cinnamon and the ½ t. ginger. Sprinkle over the apples.

3.) Now blend flour, brown sugar, ½ t. cinnamon and salt together. Cut in butter with a pastry blender or a fork until mixture looks like big crumbs. Stir in pecans.

4.) Sprinkle over apples and pat down. Bake for 35-40 minutes until nice and golden on top. Serve plain or with vanilla ice cream. Yummy for your tummy.

****

Food historians are still debating the origins of the <u>apple</u> but for the most part it is agreed that the beginning of apple cultivation began in ancient Egyptian times. The Chinese were known also to be cultivating apples at this time. In the 13th century BC, Ramses II, decreed that a variety of apples were to be cultivated in the fertile Nile Delta. As far back as the 7th century BC, the Greeks were known to be growing, harvesting and celebrating apples.

American colonists planted apple trees in the original colonies but the apple did not play a part in American history until the westward expansion began. Did you ever hear of Johnny Appleseed? He was no myth. His actual name was John Chapman. He was born in Leominster, Massachusetts on September 26, 1774. Around the turn of the 19th century, he bought apple seeds from a cider mill and headed to the Midwest where he started nurseries. In the growing frontier, new homesteaders were required to plant 50 apple trees in their first year of homesteading. To help the settlers Johnny would sell seeds and help the pioneers in growing their trees.

He didn't actually travel across America planting apple trees like some the of legends say he did. Johnny owned huge tracts of land in Ohio and Indiana which is where he settled. He primarily spread apples by selling and giving settlers trees.

Here are a few fun facts about apples:

*apple trees take 4-5 years to produce fruit

*an average tree can produce 42# of apples in a growing season

*Americans eat about 65 fresh apples a year

*25% of an apple is air

*10,000 varieties are grown worldwide, 7,000 of those varieties are grown in the US (hmm, I only know of 12)

One medium apple contains only 80 Calories, has no Fat, Sodium, or Cholesterol, has 170 mg. Potassium and 5g. Fiber.

You know how the old saying goes, "An apple a day, keeps the doctor away." A good tip I got from a friend's son is if you have indigestion at night, eat a slice of apple and it goes away. It works. I've tried it many times. Thanks, Garrett.

MOLASSES SPICE COOKIES
(Makes 4 dozen)

My favorite dessert is cookies with a cup of REALLY good coffee. If you are trying to sell your house, need a hug or are craving cookies, I recommend this recipe. The aroma that drifts around your house as these bake, will make the hardest situation seem manageable. Give yourself a time-out, collect your thoughts and know what a gift your life is. After a couple of these cookies, you'll get a new perspective on life or maybe the answer you were looking for. Big hug! Ain't life grand?

1 C. butter, softened	½ C. vegetable shortening
1 1/3 C. sugar	2 eggs
2/3 C. molasses	4 C. flour
½ C. whole wheat pastry flour	2 rounded t. each; ginger and
1 t. ground cloves	cinnamon
1 t. salt	2 t. baking soda
Sugar for coating	2 t. baking powder

1.) Preheat oven to 350 degrees. Cream butter and vegetable shortening together. Beat until light and fluffy.

2.) Add sugar, eggs and molasses. Blend thoroughly.

3.) Sift flours, cinnamon, ginger, cloves, baking soda, baking powder and salt together. Slowly add to wet ingredients. Mix well but not too much, otherwise you'll have "tough cookies." ha ha ha ha ha

4.) Form dough into balls the size of a walnut. Roll in additional sugar and place on an un-greased cookie sheet.

5.) Bake for 10-12 minutes. Less baking time...chewier cookie, longer baking time...crispier cookie. It all depends on how you like them. Now go put your feet up and take a deep breath. See, I told you things would look better.

(I realize the following quote doesn't have anything to do with this recipe BUT, it's so funny, I had to put it somewhere.)

"CONDENSED MILK IS WONDERFUL.
I JUST DON'T SEE HOW THEY CAN
GET A COW TO SIT DOWN
ON THOSE LITTLE CANS."
-Fred Allen

The Brits call <u>molasses</u>, treacle which I think I've seen in Winnie-the-Pooh books but never knew what it was. The Japanese call it kuro mitsu which means black honey. I love molasses. The flavor is intense and rich. There is nothing like it. A century ago it was the sweetener of choice because it was so inexpensive. People used to buy it by the gallon. Today the molasses you have stored in the back of your pantry is used mostly in gingerbread or baked beans.

True molasses is made from juice extracted from sugar cane stalks and boiled to a thick syrup. In the 1600's molasses was shipped from the West Indies to New England to make rum. Blackstrap molasses is the thickest and strongest of all. Because of its slightly bitter taste, which I frankly don't find bothersome, it's too robust for some recipes. I wouldn't use blackstrap molasses in gingerbread but I have used it in my homemade BBQ sauce and it is fabulous.

After WWI, the price of refined sugar dropped a great deal. This caused molasses to fall out of favor as the sweetener of choice. By 1919 the U.S. consumption of white sugar was twice what it was in the late 1800's. Today the price of molasses is TWICE that of refined white sugar. Hmmm!

In January, 1919, a two-million gallon vat of molasses exploded at the purity Distilling Company in Boston, Massachusetts. It was known as the Great Molasses Flood because that explosion sent a 30 foot wave of molasses, traveling at 35 mph, into the surrounding streets. Twenty-one people were killed and many buildings were destroyed.

Molasses is still used to make rum but it's also used in cattle feed. Actually those must be pretty healthy cows because molasses is loaded with all kinds of minerals. It is high in Manganese, which is important in the breakdown of amino acids and in the production of energy. It also contains a lot of Copper, Iron, Calcium and Potassium. It is a healthy sweetener because the nutrients have not been stripped from it. Two teaspoons of blackstrap molasses provides more Iron than 4 oz. of red meat with fewer Calories and no Fat.

When you are shopping for it, look for un-sulphured molasses in case you are sensitive to that chemical AND because the flavor of the molasses is much cleaner. Do some experimenting with it. I wonder if a tablespoon of it would be good for people with, "iron poor blood." Hmmmm....again.

DOUBLE CHOCOLATE SILK CAKE
(Makes 12-18 very rich servings)

My Grandma Elsie made the most heavenly chocolate cake with chocolate frosting. When she died, her recipe went with her. My sister-in-law and I tried to make it once to surprise my Dad, but an elephant was lighter than that attempt. For years I forgot about it. One night I had a dream about my Grandma. I was sitting on the stool in her kitchen watching her make that cake. When I woke up, I was determined to create a chocolate cake that would be worthy of her. This is not her recipe but my family thinks it is the most divine chocolate cake on the planet. This is my tribute to both of my grandmothers who inspired me in so many ways. I made so many of these cakes over a two month period I thought my friends and family would explode from chocolate overdose. However, my daughter-in-law, Leah, assures me there is no such thing. Ha ha ha!

7 oz. bittersweet chocolate, melted and slightly cooled

1 C. butter, softened

3 eggs

2 t. vanilla

½ C. unsweetened cocoa powder, I use Droste

3 t. baking powder

1 ¼ C. brown sugar, packed

1 C. buttermilk

1 T. instant coffee granules

1 1/3 C. flour

½ t. salt

Chocolate Silk Frosting Recipe, next page

1.) Butter two 9-inch cake pans, not 8-inch, 9-inch. I use the wrappers from the sticks of butter. They work great. Please don't use cooking spray it can leave a sticky residue on your pans that's hard to get off. Besides you won't believe the flavor when you use butter in this step.

2.) Melt the chocolate in a microwave or over a double boiler. Set aside to cool.

3.) Beat butter and brown sugar together until they are light and fluffy, about 2 minutes. Add eggs one at a time. Mix thoroughly.

4.) Stir in buttermilk, vanilla, instant coffee granules and the melted chocolate. Mix until well blended, about a minute.

5.) On a piece of waxed paper or parchment paper, sift together the cocoa powder, flour, baking powder and salt. With your mixer on low, slowly add the dry ingredients. Scrape the bowl down a couple times to make sure all the ingredients are incorporated. Don't over mix. Go ahead. Take a taste.

6.) OK, now stop. You need to save some batter for the cake pans.

7.) Pour the batter into your prepared cake pans, making sure to have equal amounts in both pans. Smooth the batter out.

8.) Bake in a 300-degree oven for 25-30 minutes or until a toothpick comes out clean when you insert it in the center. This is a very dense cake. If you try to take it out of the pans too soon, the cake could break. Cool, in the pans, for about 30 minutes. Remove from pans and cool completely on a wire rack.

Chocolate Silk Frosting:

Don't make this frosting until the cake is ready to be frosted. The frosting sets up like fudge and is almost impossible to spread once it's set up. If that does happen (it happened to me once) you can nuke it for about 30-45 seconds. It changes the texture of the frosting but it still tastes great. It will be more like a glaze instead of fudge-y.

8 oz. cream cheese, at room temperature

2 T. butter, softened

1 t. vanilla

¼ t. salt

¼ C. unsweetened cocoa powder

2 ½ C. powdered sugar

3.5 oz bittersweet chocolate, melted

2 t. instant coffee

1.) Beat the cream cheese and butter together. Add vanilla and salt.

2.) Sift the cocoa and powdered sugar together. Slowly add to the cream cheese mixture. Now add the melted chocolate and instant coffee.

3.) Once all the ingredients are completely mixed, turn your beaters on high for a minute. Taste. Chocolate heaven!!!

4.) Frost the cake. If you aren't going to serve this cake right away, cover it and put it in the refrigerator.

5.) You'll want to serve rather small pieces of this because it's very rich. I think it will soon become one of your favorite cakes. I surprised myself...I'm not a cake person, but I really love this one.

SORRY...THERE IS NO FEATURED INGREDIENT FOR THIS RECIPE.

Chapter 10

Teas and Other Diddies

"Help yourself"

TEA AND OTHER DIDDIES

I decided to change the format of this final chapter because I want to invite you to, "sit and talk a while." I am sharing information below that some people might not agree with. That's OK. It is the way I live. They are my choices and I am just sharing with you what I have learned and tried on myself. In no way do I expect to become anyone's medicine woman or to take the place of your doctor. That is not my intention. This chapter is all about sharing...giving out bits of information that could help you on your own journey. Take what you will and leave the rest. Just know this...I love that we are cozied up here talking like new friends and getting to know each other better.

All the recipes in this chapter will be in bold print and there will be no featured ingredient. So...when you are looking for a particular blend of herbs for a specific tea or other diddie, it will just pop out at you. Of course they will also be listed in the table of contents or index. For each recipe I will tell you how I developed it and why.

OK, first off, about my relationship to tea, herbal and otherwise. As a child I only drank "regular tea" (which shall remain nameless) when I had the flu. I was not raised with any other kind of tea. The box sat in my mother's cupboard getting older and older. Therefore, my early tea recollections were "old tea=the flu." No wonder I never drank the stuff.

I was somewhere in my mid-thirties, when my friend Susan, gave me a hot, steaming cup of apricot tea. To say I was charmed, was an understatement. In fact I was so captivated, she gave me her extra box of apricot tea, just to shut me up. That was the beginning of my extreme love of tea. Today, I have more than 40 varieties on hand at any given time. Some are packaged teas that I find on various excursions, while others are concoctions I have blended from herbs I grow or get at the health food store.

I have become so enamored with tea I started collecting tea pots so I could give tea parties. I am blessed with an abundance of very special friends, most of whom also love tea. One cold January, I decided to give a High Tea for some of them to express my gratitude that they are such an important and integral part of my life. I sent out fancy invitations, telling them to "dress up and wear a hat." Also they were each to bring some tea-type dish to pass and be at my house at 4 o'clock, sharp! I would provide the tea, the ambiance and freshly baked scones. There were six or seven of us at that first tea. I cannot explain to you how special that day was for all of us.

We have had many teas since then. One time there were 14 of us around a table that usually seats 8. We didn't care. No one noticed that we were squished in. I remember that tea because Esther wore a Goofy (Disney) hat, and Karen had to borrow one of mine because she forgot to bring one of her own. Everyone came at 4:00 pm on the dot. We drank ten pots of tea, laughed and ate and laughed some more. No one moved until 7:30 when we all realized at once, that we needed to go to the bathroom. It's a good thing I have three.

I have introduced tea to my grandchildren. John, has a particular fondness for tea. One day he was over while I was working on this cookbook. He asked if he could make a recipe for the book. "Of course, honey," I replied, "what would you like to create?" I was thinking, he really wouldn't stay interested in this latest project and get involved in something else. Shame on me for having such low expectations of my sweet John. John created **Fruit Tea** which is absolutely delicious and easy as pie. Following is his recipe for **John's Fruit Tea**: **Start with three quarts of freshly brewed sun tea, our first batch was**

Apple Cinnamon. If you've never made sun tea it is very easy. Get a clear, glass gallon jar with a lid or go to the store and buy a glass, not plastic, sun tea jar. Add three quarts of purified water and put in 3-4 tea bags (your choice of any flavor you want). Put the jar in the sun for at least three hours. On hot, summer days it brews up fast. (When I put my first batch of the year out, in March, it takes all day.) You can also do the same thing overnight in the fridge if you don't want to use the sun to "power" your tea.

When you've got your freshly made tea, add one quart of organic fruit juice. With the Apple Cinnamon Tea, we added apple juice. You could also have added part apple and part orange juice. Get creative. Serve over lots of ice. Garnish with a sprig of fresh mint or slices of apple. Do you see how creative you and your kids/grandkids could be with this? It's also a way to give them something to drink without lots of sugar. Here are some of the other tea/juice blends we came up with, just to give you an idea of what else you could do. I'm sure you'll come up with lots of your own. **Black Cherry Tea with orange or pineapple juice or cherry cider, Peach Tea with lemonade or limeade, Strawberry Kiwi Tea with half strawberry nectar and half pineapple juice and Orange Spice Tea with orange juice and lots of orange slices in the glass with the ice.** It's a great way to get your kids to drink something that's good for them and to introduce them to tea.

When I was in Boulder, Colorado, five or six years ago, a girlfriend and I decided to take the Celestial Seasonings' free tour. I learned a lot about tea from them. The tour is family-friendly, you can have a great healthy lunch in their "Celestial Café," plus you can visit their gift shop which is so much fun and has some new teas that you probably won't have back home. I had such a good time, I took two of my grandkids there when I was back in the area three years later. Celestial Seasonings can be kind of tricky to find. You can give them a call at (303) 581-1202 if you are going to be in the area or visit them on-line. Their website gives you great directions, times they are open and tells you to make a reservation if you are coming in a group of eight or more. It's way out on the outskirts of Boulder but IT IS SO WORTH THE DRIVE. Have fun!

Another aspect of my venture into tea was the herbal aspect. I was fascinated by the healing power of plants. My friend, Susan, and I took an herbal cooking class at the local college, from a Master Gardener. At the time I was only growing mint in my backyard. The instructor introduced us to fresh dill, garlic and oregano blended in cream cheese and spread on crackers, rosemary mint jelly and tea made from peppermint. I was hooked...BIG TIME. That Christmas, Susan made me an herbal vinegar with basil she had grown. The world of herbs had thrown its door wide open to me and I leaped through.

I took herb classes from Cindy, a Native Indian woman, who was a walking encyclopedia of plants that heal. She introduced me to my first Rosemary Gladstar book, Herbal Healing for Women. Rex Adam's, Miracle Medicine Foods, was my other herbal bible. I have no clue how many medicinal herbal books I have today, but I could start a small library, I'm sure. As I mentioned in the recipe for "Chris' International Pasta," parsley was the herb that healed a recurring bladder infection. This fascinated me. There were other factors involved with the healing too.

As I was trying to get rid of this infection, I was told to drink cranberry juice but there was no mention of staying away from sugar. I was taking the medication and drinking lots of cranberry juice. Two days after I stopped the medication, the infection was back with a vengeance. I learned that the cranberry juice I was drinking was loaded with sugar and sugar feeds yeast. Guess what is the cause of a bladder infection? Yeast! The whole time I was feeding the infection while I was on the medication. Most people who've tried cranberry juice say it does not work. It does...if it's unsweetened. I know, I know...YUK! Well the trick is this. If you are trying to get rid of a bladder infection...**stay away from sugar.** Make the **parsley tea, as directed in the research part of Chris' International Pasta and drink unsweetened cranberry juice, diluted with water (7 parts water to one part cranberry juice) two to three 8 oz. glasses a day.** The first day, you might not feel much better, depending on how bad the infection is. Hold on...herbs work differently than medicine. The herbs are doing their thing. Be patient. By the third day, you should be feeling close to your old self...no bloating, no lower back pain and no bladder doing the rumba. This has worked for a lot of women I know...I hope it works for you too.

It was full-steam-ahead as far as herbs were concerned by this time. One early spring day, I decided it would be a good thing to cleanse my blood. I'd been studying various herbal cleanses and decided decontaminating my blood would be a good place to start. I researched for weeks and weeks which herbs would be the most beneficial, yet would be gentle with no fear of toxic buildup. In other words, I wanted to use herbs that would make my blood clean and fresh, but I didn't want to worry about poisoning myself, since I was going to be my own guinea pig.

I came up with, what I believe to be the perfect combination. I call it **Liver/Blood Cleanse Tea** because, one of the side benefits I discovered, is it scours out your liver too. I drank 2-3 cups a week for the first two weeks. I added spearmint, from my garden, which gave it a soothing taste so I never had to choke it down. Ever since I was a child, I have battled croup. Normally, you outgrow it when you get older. I did not. I'm a young grandmother and still had bouts of croup every spring and fall. That spring, for the first time in forever, my bout with croup only lasted 3 days and was very mild. At the time I did not attribute it to the tea. I was hoping to improve

287

the clarity of my skin and eager for renewed energy. After several weeks of drinking it, my skin did have a much more radiant look and my energy level was excellent.

Because it can get very hot during the summer in Northern Illinois and the longest I ever take any herbal concoction (even the gentle ones) is 6 weeks, I did not drink any of the tea during the summer. However, I got an urge to start up again in September of that same year. Again, I drank about 2-3 cups a week, for a month. After that, I would have an occasional cup because I liked it. It wasn't until January that I realized for the first time in my life, I did not have croup in October and November! I had felt so good and been so busy, I never thought about it, not once, until much later. I started thinking about what I was doing that was different from before. I wondered if it could be the tea. I drank no more tea until the end of winter.

Toward the beginning of March I started drinking 2-3 cups a week, like I did in the fall. Sure enough, I did not get croup again in the spring. I had been croup-free for a year!!! I started sharing it with friends who had allergies, or were feeling run down. By cleaning and building up the blood, at the very least, you'll just plain old feel better and maybe have more energy. OK, OK...here's the recipe: <u>Liver/Blood Cleanse Tea</u>   3 parts mint, 2 parts nettles, 2 parts red clover, 1 part dandelion root, and 1 part astragalus. When I say part, I mean, unit of measure. For example, if you are using a 1/4 C. measuring cup, that would be your unit of measure. One part=1/4 C., 2 parts=1/2 C., 3 parts=3/4 C. Got it? Good. You could use a peanut butter jar as a unit of measure. Just as long as that unit is the same throughout the whole recipe. . Put 2 t. of the mixture in a tea ball, put the tea ball in your favorite mug, and fill the mug with boiling water. The water must be boiling for the herbs to release their healing ingredients. Don't bother trying to heat your water in the microwave. Doing it that way can be dangerous if the water gets too hot. If, on the other hand, the water doesn't get hot enough, the healing power of the herbs won't be released. Let the herbs steep in your cup for 5-10 minutes. The root parts of herbs need a longer steeping time than the leaves and flowers. If you need honey, put a little in. No white sugar, please.

I think it would be helpful to explain what each of these herbs do so you will get a basic understanding of just how this tea can benefit your body. I used the Mint as a flavoring but it also aids in digestion, relieves bloating due to gas, and helps colic.

Nettles, also called Stinging Nettles, (which is why I order them from an herb farm and don't grow them myself), are considered a cleansing herb and good for the circulatory system. They are loaded with Vitamin C. Nettle tea has been used for centuries to treat asthma.

Red Clover is another cleansing herb as well as a diuretic, which helps flush the toxins out of your system. Red clover tea, made with about 3 teaspoons of the dried flowers, can stop a bad cough in its tracks and is such a friend to your liver, your liver will throw you a party in gratitude.

Dandelion root acts as a cleansing tonic to the liver and one of the best sources of Potassium on the planet. It has been used to treat diabetes and liver diseases by European herbalists for centuries. Just a little idea I use…in the spring… if you can find a field that has not been sprayed, pick a bunch of young tender dandelion greens and throw them in a salad with your favorite vinaigrette dressing. It will clean all the winter sludge out of your blood, your skin will look fantastic and your eyes will radiate good health.

Astragalus is a Chinese herb, huang qi, that has been used for over 2,000 years in traditional Chinese medicine. The healing part of the plant is the root.

When I got my first order, it looked like a bunch of rough tongue depressors. I cut each piece into smaller pieces and grind it up in my herb grinder (which is really just a small coffee grinder that I use exclusively for herbs). It is one of the best immune builders I know of. When the flu season came on strong and early this year, I made astragalus tea, flavored with anise hyssop, for my husband and I. We did not get sick. People were hacking and wheezing all around us...we drank more tea. It is wonderful for resisting diseases and infections. Many studies are being done as to its beneficial effects on people who are going through chemo therapy. Why not get out there and do some research of your own? You'll be amazed at what you can learn.

Once I experimented with **Liver Cleanse Tea**, I started growing more herbs to develop other teas. I was having a ball. I researched constantly and called Cindy frequently. The next tea I created was <u>**Lung Tea**</u>. It's a soothing tea, if like me, your colds tend to settle in your chest. The recipe is as follows: 1 T. rose hips, ground up, 2 T. borage leaves and flowers, 2 T. echinacea root, 2 T. astragalus, 3 T. nettles, and 4 T. mint. Use only dried herbs. Blend together. You can easily double or triple this recipe depending on how much you think you'll need. The recipe above is just for a week. Following is an explanation of the benefits of these herbs , but I won't repeat the ones I have explained previously:

<u>Rose Hips</u>, are loaded with Vitamin C. If you have any rose bushes growing in your yard, rose hips are the little red berry-like pods that develop after the petals have fallen off the rose. Deer love them. You should too, if they have not been sprayed. Cut them off the bush and dry them thoroughly. Put them in a glass jar and they'll keep nicely over the winter. They are nature's purest Vitamin C "tablet." I've eaten them straight off the bush. They don't taste like much, and they're chewy, but they are really good for you. If you do any hiking, you might notice them on wild rose bushes in the woods and along the

paths where you walk. You can always get them from your health food store if you don't have them growing near you.

Borage, grows all over in my garden. If I forget to pick off the seed heads...watch out...borage plants are everywhere. They will easily reseed from year to year, so once it starts in your garden you will never have to buy another borage plant. In fact, your herby friends will be coming to you to get plants for their own gardens. Borage is a beautiful plant that can grow to about 3-4 feet tall in good soil. It has the prettiest blue star-shaped flowers, which I love to use on edible flower tea sandwiches or in salads. Among ancient cultures borage had a reputation for summoning courage. Ancient Celtic warriors would drink a wine flavored with borage before heading into battle. Upon drinking the wine, they would feel euphoric which would then make their fears disappear. It is felt that it was probably the wine, not the borage, that was the great fear-dissipater. Modern herbalists use borage to relieve fevers, bronchitis, sore throats and diarrhea. Because it helps bring mucous up from the lungs, I use it in this tea.

Echinacea, has recently become a very popular but greatly overused herb. You should not take echinacea for more than two to three weeks. It's not that it will hurt you, it's just that its effectiveness will be greatly reduced because your body has gotten used to it. Use it only as you need it, not as a preventative measure. Echinacea is more commonly know as purple coneflower. You might even have some growing in your perennial garden. It is the root of the plant that has all the healing power. Native Indians discovered its power to heal poisonous snake bites long ago. Today it is used for fighting sore throats, ear infections, bronchitis, minor burns, allergies, viral infections, and even toothaches. Pretty powerful herb, wouldn't you say? The rest of the herbs in this tea, **Mint, Nettles and Astragalus** were all discussed in **Liver Cleanse Tea.**

291

The next tea I discovered unintentionally but I wish I knew about it when I was a teenager. I have had severe menstrual cramps forever. When I was in high school, I'd get a pass from the teacher to go to the nurse's office and lie down on one of the million cots in her office, to curl up and just groan...along with a million of my female counterparts. If you are one of the lucky ones to never have had to go through this...get down on your knees immediately and thank God. My mother was sympathetic but my doctor was not. He just thought I was being female. Anyone who has experienced this knows how debilitating they can be.

When I went away to college, my heating pad was passed around the dorm, as needed. I remember my roommate, who had never had a menstrual cramp in her life, thought sit ups might help. Even though I did them every night, I was skeptical they might be helpful at this time. I dragged myself off the bed, lay on the floor like a piece of limp bacon and proceeded to do three sit ups. I immediately threw up. Sit ups don't help.

When I was a newlywed, my doctor put me on some medication for abdominal surgery. For the first time, I was cramp free. Oh joy! However, the price for this ecstasy was pretty high. In fact, that's what I was...high. I could not feel anything from the waist down. My new husband and I were shopping at a big mall near our apartment. I had just taken one of the "no cramp pills." I was giggling and laughing about not being able to feel the lower half of my body but I could definitely see my legs. I thought this was very funny and started twirling in Marshall Fields. My husband was mortified. He was concerned and embarrassed all at the same time. I tried a half a pill the next time...I never took them again after that.

Birth control pills helped; having a baby helped some more. I still had bad cramps once in a while though. I was sick and tired of feeling like a slug every month. UGH! I started researching natural alternatives. I discovered taking a Calcium Magnesium supplement helped a lot but Cramp Tea was the frosting on the cake. It has a wonderful lemony taste and works so subtly, your cramps are gone before you realize it. It takes about a half hour before they are all gone but the tea works. It really works. My daughter-in-law was visiting one time. My son came into the kitchen and asked me if I had something to help her...she was miserable and embarrassed to ask me herself. Immediately I made some Cramp Tea for her. Within a half hour she was asleep and woke up feeling great. Here is my most excellent recipe for this tea. I hope it helps you too. WARNING: This should not be taken during pregnancy!

Cramp Tea recipe: 2 parts raspberry leaf, 2 parts motherwort and 2 parts lemon verbena. I use a half cup measure to equal one part because I always want this tea on hand. Put 2 teaspoons in your tea ball, pour boiling water over and let it steep for 5-7 minutes. You will love the smell of this tea as much as the taste. But mostly you will love how it gently carries away those cramps before you even realize it's happened. Don't forget to help yourself even more by taking that Calcium Magnesium supplement...a good one.

<u>Raspberry Leaf</u> is an easy one to find, especially if you have red raspberry bushes in your own yard. Bet you didn't know you had a medicinal bush growing right next to your vegetable garden did you? Yep, this is where my raspberry leaves come from. Raspberries are one of my favorite fruit. Not only do my bushes give me luscious red raspberries, but they provide me with a key ingredient for this tea. Pick the leaves in late spring and early summer, before the fruit forms. The healing properties are stronger then because the energy won't be going toward producing fruit. Don't strip your bushes either. A Native rule is to pick one leaf and leave seven, therefore allowing Nature to always have the ability to regenerate.

Raspberry leaf is known to help relax the uterus so **don't use this during pregnancy.** Raspberry has a toning effect that helps women's reproductive systems function normally. It can also help in stopping heavy menstrual bleeding. I just use it for cramps. It is such a blessed relief.

Motherwort is a uterine stimulant. It can be used during labor but not during pregnancy. The alkaloids in the leaves, flowers and stems encourage and ease uterine contractions. That's why it works so well on cramps.

Lemon Verbena is one of my favorite herbs of all time. I use it in cookies, salads, salad dressing, herbal vinegars and on those little tea sandwiches I was talking about. It is a tender perennial, so it does not survive Chicago winters. I tried bringing a pot of it in, several times but it does not do well. It definitely likes to be outside. I grow a big pot of it on my deck every summer. About halfway through the season, I prune it to half its size. It seems to love that. By September it is in full bloom. I use the dried leaves to make the tea. When you crush the leaves, the most fragrant lemon aroma fills the air. Sigh. Lemon verbena is not well known medicinally, but mostly as an aromatic. It does have a calming effect, like a sedative, and is used to reduce fevers. It is in this tea, as much for its flavor, as well as its ability to soothe.

Here's an easy little herbal trick you might want to attempt. If you have a favorite pound cake recipe try this once and see how you like it. Lay a few sprig tips of fresh lemon verbena in the bottom of your prepared cake pan. Make the sprigs lie down as flat as you can. Pour the batter over the herbs and bake like you normally would. When you take the cake out of the pan, you will have the beautiful herb imprinted on the top of your cake. Your friends and your family will be very impressed. You can even finely chop seven or eight of the leaves before baking and stir them into the batter. It's a good variation instead of lemon peel.

If you really want to go all out, you can make a **Lemon Syrup** to pour on the pound cake:

Blend 1/4 C. honey, 5 T. butter, 2 T. fresh lemon juice and 2 t. chopped verbena leaves. Heat this up on the stove. Bring to a low simmer, then let it gently bubble away for 2-3 minutes to let the lemon verbena infuse the butter and honey. Serve the syrup on the side in a small pitcher. Drizzle it over the warm cake. See what that does to your family's taste buds. This is also good on pancakes, waffles or French toast. I've even been known to drizzle a little over fresh strawberries. Pure heaven!

So here it is...the end of my first cookbook. I can't believe over eight years of love and fun and sometimes frustration have lead me to this point. I hope you enjoy **Cooking with Spirit**. It has taken me on an incredible journey of self-discovery. When I started this book I had no idea what I was doing, I just wanted to share great food and pass around a big helping of love. I'm looking forward to meeting some of you. Thanks. BIG HUG! Jasmine Rose

Bibliography

"A Brief History of Wine." Honey Creek Vineyard. 23 Aug. 2004. <www.honeycreek.us/history.htm>.

"A Short History of Apples." Ricker Hill Orchards. 20 Mar. 2002. <www.rickerhill.com/apple>.

"A Short History of Vinegar." Cipriani. 11 Mar. 2003. <www.cipriani.com>.

"All About Tomatoes." What's Cooking America. 29 Mar. 2005. <www.whatscookingamerica.net/tomato>.

Allen, Zel & Reuben. "An Apple a Day Keeps the Doctor Away." Vegetarian Paradise. 20 Mar. 2002. <www.vegparadise.com/highestperch39.html>.

Allen, Zel & Reuben. "Cabbage Takes a Roller Coaster Ride." Vegetarian Paradise. 23 Jul. 2003. <www.vegparadise.com/highestperch33.html>.

Allen, Zel & Reuben. "Going Bananas." Vegetarian Paradise. 21 Apr. 2005. <www.vegparadise.com/highestperch42.html>.

Allen, Zel & Reuben. "High Flying Barley Crashes in Modern Times." Vegetarian Paradise. 1 Jul. 2002. <www.vegparadise.com/highestperch410.html>.

Allen, Zel & Reuben. "Humongous Fungus Among Us." Vegetarian Paradise. 11 Mar. 2007. <www.vegparadise.com/highestperch34.html>.

Allen, Zel & Reuben. "Taming the Wild Strawberry." Vegetatian Paradise. 19 Jul. 2006. <www.vegparadise.com/highest perch45.html>.

Allen, Zel & Reuben. "The Sweet Potato Myth." <u>Vegetarian Paradise.</u> 3 Feb. 2007. <<u>www.vegparadise.com/highestperch11html</u>>.

Allen, Zel & Reuben. "Zucchini-Summer's Abundant Delight." <u>Vegetarian Paradise.</u> 1 Aug. 2003. <<u>www.vegparadise.com/highestperch7. html</u>>.

Bader, Myles H. <u>Grandmother's Kitchen Wisdom.</u> Philadelphia, Pennsylvania: Mylin Publishing, 1999.

"Cheddar Gorge & Cheddar Caves." <u>Cheddar Village & Gorge.</u> 15 Sep. 2004. <<u>www.cheddarsomerset.co.uk</u>>.

Chef Brad. "Cumin." <u>Olde Time Cooking & Nostalgia.</u> 17 Nov. 2007. <<u>www.oldetimecooking.com/cumin</u>>.

"Cilantro." <u>Gourmet Sleuth.com.</u> 4 Aug. 2002. <<u>www.gourmetsleuth.com/cilantro.htm</u>>.

Conant, Patricia. "Bulghur & Cracked Wheat." <u>The Epicurean Table.</u> 26 Jul. 2005. <<u>www.epicureantable.com</u>>.

Cox, Sam. "I Say Tomayto, You Say Tomahto." <u>Colorado State.Edu.</u> 29 Mar. 2005. <<u>www.lamar/colostate.edu/~samcox/tomato.html</u>>.

Coyle, L. P. <u>The World Encyclopedia of Food.</u> New York, N.Y. Facts on File, Inc., 1982.

Damrosch, Barbara. "Celery Cultivation & History." <u>Kalamazoo County, MI.</u> 29 Apr. 2003. <<u>www.rootsweb.ancestry.com/!~milalama/celery.htm</u>>.

Duke, James A. <u>The Green Pharmacy.</u> Emmaus, Pennsylvania: Rodale Press, 1997.

Dunne, Lavon J. Nutrition Almanac. Fifth. Ed. David E. Fogarty. New York, NY: McGraw-Hill, 2002.

"Fertile Crescent." Answers.com. 1 Jul. 2002. <www.answers.com/topic/fertile-crescent>.

Filippone, Peggy T. "Honey History." Home Cooking. 11 Nov. 2004. <www.homecooking.about.com/od/ foodhistory/a/honeyhistory.htm>.

Filippone, Peggy T. "Molasses History." Homecooking. 15 Oct. 2007. <www.homecooking.about.com/ foodhistory/molasses>.

Filippone, Peggy T. "Mushroom History." Homecooking. 13 Mar. 2007. <www.homecooking.about.com/ foodhistory/shroomhist>.

Florida Fresh Tomato Committee. "The Well-Traveled Tomato." Fabulous Foods.Com. 29 Mar. 2005. <www.fabulousfoods.com/features>.

Fowler, Damon L., ed. Dining at Monticello. United Kingdom: Butler & Tanner, 2005.

Grieve, M. "Apple." Botanical.com. 20 Mar. 2002. <www.botanical.com/apple>.

Hagen, Alan T. "Amaranth." Walton Feed. 25 Aug. 2001. <www.waltonfeed.com/self/amaranth. html>.

Hazen, Theodore R. "The History of Flour Milling." 16 Apr. 2004. <www.angelfire.com/journal/ millrestoration/history.html>.

Heywood, V. H., ed. Flowering Plants of the World. 2nd ed. United Kingdom: Oxford University Press, 1993.

Hirst, K. K. "Sweet Potato Domestication." About.com. 3 Feb. 2007. <www.archaeology.about.com/od/ domestications/qt/sweet_potato.htm>.

"History & Lore." University of Illinois Extension. 19 Jul. 2006. <www.urbanext.uiuc.edu/strawberries>.

"History of Chocolate." Kara. 23 Jul. 2003. <www.karachocolates.com/chochist. html>.

"History of Cucumbers." Eden Farms. 6 Aug. 2005. <www.edenfarms.com.au/cues.htm>.

"History of Olive Oil." EMOC. 11 Aug. 2003. <www.emocsyria.com/en/history.htm>.

"History of Pepper." Cedar Rock Pepper. 29 Sep. 2005. <www.cedarrockpepper.com/history. html>.

"History of the Mango." All About Mangos. 8 Jun. 2004. <www.freshmangos.com>.

Holmes, Hannah. "Why Asparagus Makes Your Pee Stink." Discovery Channel. 14 May. 2004. <www.dsc.discovery.com/guides/skinny-on/asparagus.html>.

Hudson, Jeff. "Molasses Bittersweet History." San Francisco Gate. 15 Oct. 2007. <sfgate.com/cgi-bin/article/archive>.

"Johnny Appleseed." 20 Mar. 2002. <www.appleappetite.com/Johnny.htm>.

"Key Limes." Food Reference. 23 Feb. 2005. <www.foodreference.com/html/artkey limes.html>.

"Limes." Fresh King. 23 Feb. 2005. <www.freshking.com>.

Loe, Theresa. The Herbal Home Companion. New York, N.Y. Kensington Publishing Corp., 1996.

Margen, Sheldon. The Wellness Encyclopedia of Food & Nutrition. New York, N.Y. Rebus, 1992.

Mateljan, George. "Blackstrap Molasses." World's Healthiest Foods. 15 Oct. 2007. <www.whfoods.org/genpage>.

McGovern, Patrick E., Don Glusker, and Lawrence Exner. "The Origins of Wine." University of Pennsylvania Museum of Archaeology and Anthropology. 23 Aug. 2004. <www.musuem.upenn.edu>.

Mitchell, Patricia B. "Mayo Info." Food History.Com. 30 May. 2003. <www.foodhistory.com/foodnotes/leftovers/mayo/info>.

National Garden Bureau. "2002: Year of the Spinach." 17 Apr. 2007. <www.colostate.edu/Depts/CoopExt>.

"Nutrition in a Nutshell." National Pecan Sheller Association. 10 May. 2006. <www.ilovepecans.org/nutrition3.html>.

Ody, Penelope. The Complete Medicinal Herbal. Ed. Tanya Hines. New York, N Y: DK Publishing, Inc., 1993.

"Olive Oil History." Global Gourmet. 11 Aug. 2003. <www.globalgourmet.com/food>.

"Olives." Soup Song. 29 Mar. 2005. <www.soupsong.com/olive.html>.

Ortiz, Elizabeth L. The Encyclopedia of Herb, Spices & Flavourings. Ed. Laura Washburn. London, England: Doring Kindersley Ltd., 1992.

"Parmesan (Parmigiano)" Cheese. 20 Mar. 2007. <www.cheese.com>.

Ritchie, Carson I. Food in Civilization. First. New York, N.Y. & Toronto, Canada: Beaufort Books, Inc., 1981.

Rodale Press. Illustrated Encyclopedia of Herbs. Ed. Claire Kowalchik. Emmaus, Pennsylvania: Rodale Press, 1987.

Seelig, R. A. "What is the History of Oranges." Oregon State University. 17 Jan. 2003. <www.oregonstate.edu/faq/oranges2.html>.

Skelton, Emily. "Kale: The Phytonutrient Master." Seeds of Change. 13 Sep. 2004. <www.seedsofchange.com/enewsletter/ issue_57/kaleasp>.

Spadaccini, James. "The Sweet Lure of Chocolate." Exploratorium. 23 Jul. 2003. <www.exploratorium.edu/exploring_chocolate>.

"Spinach." 17 Apr. 2007. <www.uga.edu/vegetable/spinach.html>.

"Sprout Nutrition." Sprout People. 1 Jun. 2006. <www.sproutpeople.com/nutrition.htm>.

Stadley, Linda. "Mayonnaise." What's Cooking America. 30 May. 2003. <www.whatscookingamerica.net/ history/saucehistory.htm>.

Stamets, Paul. "Mushrooms, Civilizations and History." 11 Mar. 2007. <www.shroomery.org>.

"Sunflower History." Cyber Space Farm. 3 Apr. 2004. <www.cyberspaceag.com/kansascrops.com>.

"Swiss Chard." Practically Edible. 3 Mar. 2007. <www.practicallyedible.com/ediblensf>.

Tannahill, Reay. Food in History. New York, N.Y. Stein & Day Publishers, 1973.

"Tea & Health." <u>Celestial Seasonings</u>. 5 Jun. 2004. <www.celestialseasonings.com/health>.

"The History of the Potato." <u>Essortment</u>. 20 Feb. 2002. <www.essortment.com/all/potato history_rvap.htm>.

The Origin of Bananas." <u>Bananas</u>. 21 Apr. 2005. <www.banana.com>.

Touissant, Jean-Luc. "The Walnut in Myth & History." <u>The Global Gourmet</u>. 7 May. 2003. <www.globalgourmet.com/food/special>.

"Traditional Hand Harvesting in Minnesota." <u>Northern Lakes Wild Rice Company</u>. 4 Feb. 2001. <www.northernlakeswildrice.com/ history.htm>.

Trager, James. <u>The Food Chronology</u>. First. New York, N.Y. Henry Holt & Co., 1995.

"Vanilla History." <u>Vanilla, Saffron Imports</u>. 10 Oct. 2002. <www.saffron.com/vanhistory.html>.

Vogel, Mark. "Swiss Chard." <u>Food Reference</u>. 2 Jul. 2001. <www.foodreference.com/html/art-swiss-chard.html>.

"Wild Rice.a Synopsis." <u>Chieftain Wild Rice Company</u>. 4 Feb. 2001. <www.chieftainwildrice.com/aboutus>.

Wilhelm, Stephen, and James E. Sagen. "History." <u>Manzanita Berry Farms</u>. 19 Jul. 2006. <www.berries4u.com/history.htm>.

Wood, Rebecca. <u>The Whole Foods Encyclopedia</u>. New York, N.Y. Prentiss-Hall Press, 1998.

INDEX

BREAKFAST
Blissful Fruit Salad (p.152-4)
Breakfast Fruit Puff (p.44-5)
Cerebral Pancakes (p.243-5)
Crunchy, Toasty Banana Muffins (p.234-6)
Designer Oatmeal (p.78-80)
Extra Moist Pumpkin Muffins (p.249-51)
Fiesta Bonito Burrito (p.41-3)
Fluffy Scrambled Wrap (p.55-7)
Fruits of Eden Sauce (p.258-60)
Grandma Schulze's Banana Bread (p.252-4)
Green Eggs (p.52-4)
Lemon Syrup (p.294)
Orange Pecan Scones (p.246-8)
Practically Perfect Potato Pancakes (p.119-21)
Salute to the Sunrise Eggs (p.49-51)
Sort of Corn Quiche (p.38-40)
Special Apple Pudding (p.270-2)
Strawberry Cream Muffins (p.240-2)
Swiss, Swiss Frittata (p.46-8)

DESSERT
Breakfast Fruit Puff (p.44-5)
Double Chocolate Silk Cake (p.276-8)
Fruits of Eden Sauce (p.258-60)
Gooey Chocolate Dessert Scones (p.267-9)
Grandma Nicol's Strawberry Shortcake (p.261-3)
Grandma Schulze's Banana Bread (p.252-4)
Lemon Syrup (p.294)
Molasses Spice Cookies (p.273-5)

Rainbow Parfait (p.264-6)
Special Apple Pudding (p.270-2)
Strawberry Cream Muffins (p.240-2)

FISH & SEAFOOD
Crab Louie Obispo (p.182-4)
Mary Anne's Shrimp Salad (p.147-8)
Multi-talented Tilapia Salad (p.23-5)
Serendipitous Shrimp Salad (p.155-7)
Slippery Salmon with a Bite (p.9-10)
Verde Sole (p.20-22)

MAIN COURSES
Au Gratin Potato Soup (p.225-7)
Garlic & Rosemary Chicken (p.17-19)
Ginger Chicken over Forbidden Rice (p.11-13)
Hawaiian Mahalo Burgers (p.29-31)
No Leftovers Turkey Trot (p.3-5)
Potato Mushroom Potage (p.210-12)
Scarlet O' Chicken (p.6-8)
Serendipitous Shrimp Salad (p.155-7)
Slippery Salmon with a Bite (p.9-10)
Slobbering Chicken (p.14-16)
Supremely Aromatic Moussaka (p.26-28)
Too Good to Be True Soup (p.213-15)
Verde Sole (p.20-22)

PASTA
Aye Karumba Pasta Salad (p.158-60)

Sunshine Salad with Orange Vinaigrette (p.149-51)
Throw Together Salad (p.197-9)
Tomato Corn Salad with Honey Lime Dressing (p.185-7)

SALAD DRESSINGS
Garlic Cilantro Dressing (p.200-1)
Ginger Garlic Salad Dressing (p.170)
Herb-y Orange Dressing (p.188)
Honey Curry Dressing (p.179)
Honey Lime Dressing (p.185)
Mustard Garlic Dressing (p.191)
New Dawn Dressing(p.183)
Orange Vinaigrette (p.149)
Raspberry Vinaigrette (p.176)

SAUCES
Curry Mayonnaise (p.30)
Fresh Tomato Basil Sauce (p.84)
Garlic Cilantro Dressing (p.200-1)

SIDE DISHES
Blissful Fruit Salad (p.152-4)
Cheesy Layered Potatoes (p.58-60)
Creamy Polka Dot Potatoes (p.97-9)
Edible Flower Tea Sandwiches (p.142-4)
Eggs-terrestrial Eggplant (P.102-3)
Enchanted Forest Risotto (p.66-8)
Forget the Peppers Casserole (p.63-5)
Gloriously Crunchy Wraps (p.139-41)
Golden Eggs n' Rice (p.35-7)

Grilled Zucchini Cheese Sandwiches (p.136-38)
Heavenly Green Beans (p.110-12)
Honey Glazed Carrots (p.95-6)
Karen & Frank's Stuffed 'Shrooms (p.86-8)
Peek-a-Boo Cauliflower (p.113-5)
Potato Butternut Mash (p.100-1)
Practically Perfect Potato Pancakes (p.119-21)
Quick As a Wink Salad (p.167-9)
Rainbow Stir Fry (p.107-09)
Red & Green Salad with Toasted Almonds (p.170-2)
Sort of Corn Quiche (p.38-40)
Summer Squash Ecstasy (p.92-4)
Swiss, Swiss Frittata (p.46-8)
Wonder Beans (p.116-8)
Woo-Dee-Woo Vegetables (p.89-91)

SOUP

Au Gratin Potato Soup (p.225-7)
Golden Cauliflower Soup (p.219-21)
Happy Soup (p.207-09)
Merlin's Magical Mushroom Medley (p.204-6)
My Most Comforting Soup (p.222-4)
Potato Mushroom Potage (p.210-12)
Smokey Kale Soup with Bow Ties (p.228-30)
South of the Border Lentil Stew (p.216-8)
Too Good to Be True Soup (p.213-15)

VEGETARIAN MAIN COURSES

VEGETARIAN MAIN COURSES (cont.)

Summer Squash Ecstasy (p.92-4)

Swiss, Swiss Frittata (p.46-8)

Throw Together Salad (p.197-9)

Unforgettable Bulgur Casserole (p.75-7)

Printed in the United States
132084LV00005B/19/P